T0005787

DEATH PREFERS THE MINOR KEYS

DEATH PREFERS THE MINOR KEYS

~

Sean Thomas Dougherty

AMERICAN POETS CONTINUUM SERIES, NO. 202

BOA EDITIONS, LTD. ~ ROCHESTER, NY ~ 2023

First Edition
23 24 25 26 7 6 5 4 3 2 1

For information about permission to reuse any material from this book, please contact
The Permissions Company at www.permissionscompany.com or e-mail permdude@
gmail.com.

Publications by BOA Editions, Ltd.—a not-for-profit corporation under section 501
(c) (3) of the United States Internal Revenue Code—are made possible with funds
from a variety of sources, including public funds from the Literature Program of the
National Endowment for the Arts; the New York State Council on the Arts, a state
agency; and the County of Monroe, NY. Private funding sources include the Max
and Marian Farash Charitable Foundation; the Mary S. Mulligan Charitable Trust;
the Rochester Area Community Foundation; the Ames-Amzalak Memorial Trust in
memory of Henry Ames, Semon Amzalak, and Dan Amzalak; the LGBT Fund of
Greater Rochester; and contributions from many individuals nationwide. See Colophon
on page 146 for special individual acknowledgments.

Cover Design: Sandy Knight
Cover Art: Hoop Dreams by Anne Havens
Interior Design and Composition: Isabella Madeira
BOA Logo: Mirko

BOA Editions books are available electronically through BookShare, an online dis-
tributor offering Large-Print, Braille, Multimedia Audio Book, and Dyslexic formats,
as well as through e-readers that feature text to speech capabilities.

Cataloging-in-Publication Data is available from the Library of Congress.

BOA Editions, Ltd.
250 North Goodman Street, Suite 306
Rochester, NY 14607
www.boaeditions.org
A. Poulin, Jr., Founder (1938-1996)

State of the Arts
NYSCA

NATIONAL
ENDOWMENT
for the ARTS
arts.gov

Contents

1

Death Letter #2

I'm not sure where I left it. In the fruit aisle beside the avocadoes and the kiwis. On the ledge of a quarry bank three decades ago. I lost my life when she left goes every country song. When my dog died. When my beer ran out. This life, as if tied to a string. The tradition says it is not the maker but the marionettes who control the strings. But if you listen you can hear the maker simply touches them now and then, the way a mallet in a piano will touch a piano string and make a note, a vibration *sostenuto* that shudders the body. My wife points out, but if it is us who hold the strings of our fate, what if we pull them too hard, what if we snap them and lose our connection? So many of us could be walking through this life tugging at the end of a string attached to no-thing. The woman I work taking care of, she is sobbing again when I arrive for my shift. I knock lightly on the door and there she is on her bed with her large pile of thumb-worn photos of her family, holding each one, telling me who is in each photo and sobbing. Then she is ok. She looks up, can I have a cigarette she says. The simple human truth is we are tougher than we think we are even when we aren't. After we receive a word, we receive another, a set, or series of words like pieces to a puzzle we arrange. We send the words out into the world of strangers who pick up those words and place each one into a hole in their body. Each of us goes through life with these holes in our bodies until the right words find them. And then afterwards? What do we look like, this patch of quilted words with arms and legs? I cannot say. I've never seen anyone so whole. I've never seen a person pass me who wasn't leaking light. You call me from the waiting room, you left for the hospital after I left for work. I will be up all night watching over your absence. How many long nights speaking to your small face on a screen? The tradition says we can fool death by switching names or giving our children long impossible names to pronounce. Hopefully, death will never be able to pronounce Andalujza Akhmatova Dougherty. For it is a name made of names death knows so well as separate people, or perhaps he will see himself for the first time in her eyes. I need a haircut he will say and go on his way. Did you know for a long time each night you left me for the hospital I shaved my head. As if I was heading off towards my own execution. Come for me instead, I'd say to the shadow hovering at the edge of my razor. There are rituals and routines for dying, but also for living. I showed our daughter how to sit under the oak tree. I am getting a little bit bored she says. Don't you hear the birds beneath the traffic I ask her. Suddenly she jumps up, there are so many! They are everywhere! If anything, now she will go through this life knowing she is surrounded by songs. Whenever there is music, death stops to listen. If you don't believe me, watch the cat's shadow saunter through the yard, hidden by the bougainvillea. Haven't you been listening; the crow scolds me. Now they are laughing. *Caw caw*, soon we will eat. They are teasing the small songbirds and the sparrows hopping nervously in the tulip tree. The yellow finch, safe on the telephone wire, sends off a high crescendo, the robin flies away from her blue-egged nest, follow me she says. All the birds have a special song they are born with, this warning. They are death's troubadours. They sing their high-pitched notes just for his arrival. There is a kind of silence death cannot stand. The darkness between stars sends a wind-less shudder across the pages suddenly empty of names. Without life, how can there be death? In the solitude of space he comes face to face with his oblivion. This is why life is so fragile and holy to Azrael more than any other angel.

2

The Shape of a Pill

What is there if not this labor, the light labor of hands popping pills out of packages, checking names, prescription tags, double checking the correct dosage. Outside is only the dark and the near empty parking lot, the small labor of looking to make sure a sleeping man is breathing. So many shapes and colors of different pills that pass through my gloved hands. Nearly translucent gel-like amber ovals that glitter like jewels and stick to the pack, tiny white ovals that could put a man to sleep; brown pills, red pills, blue, ovals and circles so we may swallow them though some anti-anxiety drugs come in strange shapes. Buspirone with side indents like tabs, I suspect so one could break in half if needed. There are even hexagons, for high blood pressure and narcolepsy, a pill to open one's eyes. To close one's eyes, to speed up the heart's rate or slow it down, to level the blood pressure, all these different shapes for the body, for the organs, the blood, the brain. Numbered and lettered, made in giant factories. They pass through my hands. I put them in tiny cups. I mix some in yogurt, so they go down the throat and no one chokes. After I close my med cart and turn off the light, I imagine the pills glow with a light of their own: *snowlight, locomativelight, electrocardiagramlight,* the light that travels through the veins, *blueriverlight, autumnleaflight,* because the med cart wants to fly, wants to visit the old villages. It knows nothing of profit. It flies through the narrow mountain pass, wants to roll toward the bed of the woman in pain on a thin mattress, the man coughing in a mine, the barefoot child wheezing, the one who cannot sit up straight, the one lisping, the one going blind, the palsied—backwards the med cart flies, carrying all the human labor that made these pills, the chemists with their calculations, the giant corporations who paid for them. Someone needed to imagine the need, which is another way to say they diagnosed. A doctor somewhere thought up the first ailment, checked the lab work, wrote it down, all the pieces of paper, encyclopedic, calculations, compounds, formulas, and then one day the masked workers leaned over the assembly line. Thousands of hair-netted and gloved factory workers, suited executives flying first class. Because they invented a tiny pill. Placed on the tongue. Like the eucharist. For the body. For the blood. Dissolving down to the elements: magnesium, sodium, tea tree leaf, turmeric, oyster shell, what is prescribed in this life? What is taken and what is given? But where is the cure for loneliness? The med cart speaks, in a soft female voice, I have one. What is the pill for love lorn? I have one. What is the pill for grief? I have one. Is there a pill for hopelessness? I have one. Is there a pill for my father's beatings? My mother's slaps? Is there a pill for wanting to fly? A punk rock pill to replace my pacemaker? I have one. A pill to fill the cathedral hollow in my chest? I have one. A pill for exile? Evacuation? A pill to forget genocide? A *bel canto* pill to recall? A heart-shaped pill for regret? A pill the shape of a trumpet's bell? Or a tambourine, so I may shimmy and sway, though no one has ever asked me to dance. Do you have a pill to teach me how to finally spell? Words like peonies, or bourgeoise? An Episcopalian pill that smells like old money? Can you call me in that prescription? A pill so I may sing and open my diaphragm round as the Os in osteoporosis…

Written on the Back of Medical Forms

What I have to tell you here has more to do with being human than with spirit, but then what is spirit but the heart of being human? The man wakes up to piss at 2 AM. After he is done, I tell him, "Come on, let's get you back in bed." "No," he says, "I am not going back to bed." He stamps his foot, and all the dark disappears. It is so strange: these moments that feel the most familiar are the ones that feel the strangest. I clap the lights back off, take his hand, he says, "I'm not tired." "It's night," I say. I guide him gently into bed, all the while chattering about what we will do tomorrow, how he must sleep because he will see his mother, and you don't want to fall asleep visiting her. "But I am home," he says, as I pull the covers to his chin. As I tuck him in, I tell him, "No no, you are here, where I take care of you," and as his eyes close, I tell him in exquisite detail of the wonderful sausages I will fry him up for breakfast.

~

Somewhere I erred. Somewhere I forgot the cartography for going forward. I am hollow as a sewer pipe. I make notes on medical forms while you are at the hospital. Everyone in my care is sleeping easy. Then they aren't confused, thinking it is time to shower. The woman tells me she has showered at midnight, returns to her room, emerges to tell me again. "Are you ok?" I ask. "No, I'm not fucking ok!" Then she calms, "I miss my children." I remind her, "But they are grown men. You see your family more than most of us who work here." She wails, "I haven't seen them in so long!" "You just visited home yesterday. Try to remember, you had a good visit." "I hate my mother!" Now I know she just doesn't want to go back to bed. "Here. Play some cards in your room. I have meds to pass." I try not to indulge self-pity. You text me the MRI went ok.

~

Sometimes I swear this building is alive and breathing. Years ago it was a motel. The ghosts of divorced fishermen wander the halls with the residents. When it rains, everything is murmurous. What I thought was a scar was only a cloud come to rest on my wrist. My grief at your long passing hides in my marrow. When I met you, I recognized you by how you wore the rain. Or were you a willow in the wind, and I was a small bird. I never figured out if it was you or I or was it the dead trees singing? Deja Vu: It is so ironic these moments that feel the most familiar are the ones that feel the strangest. The tree that sings for the dead.

~

What is the distance between belonging and still stranger? Our blood reaches back to the same black mountains. You feel you have been there before, done it all before. How easy it is for a place to feel like home, in the city you do not speak the language except a few greetings, numbers, you grin like the village idiot, point at the word for pardon. After a few weeks, the checkout girl at the *Apoteka* recognizes your daughter in the pram, *coochicoo*, the man at the newsstand kiosk hands you your brand of cigarettes before you ask. What minor keys that haunt me. How distant is the space between friend and stranger, between foreigner and you belong? Don't be fooled. You feel you have been there before, done it again. Each night the man forgets the day. The man mistakes me for Sisyphus. The man opens the bathroom door, and I am there. "Nice job," I say. "I will help you get back in bed, you are right on schedule." He says, "I don't want to go back to bed." I say, "You always go to the bathroom at this time.

Look at the clock, it is only 1:44 AM. It is the middle of the night." His mind resets itself to distant memories. I walk him across the room and help him turn to sit on his bed, but before he swings his legs up, he stops and stiffens. His face gets all screwed up. "But why are you awake," he asks. He is emphatic. "Why do you get to stay awake?" I ask him, "Who am I?" (In this way I can judge how confused he is.) He says my name. He says it with affection. I know now he will be ok. I can guide him easily. "I watch over you," I say. "I watch over eight people while you all sleep." "Eight people!" He exclaims with honest surprise. "I stay up to make sure you are ok, that you aren't having seizures, to make sure you sleep well." "When I wake up will you sleep then?" "No, I will help you when you wake, then make you breakfast." "But what," he says, "if I never wake up? What if—" "Shhh, I will wake you." I lay him back on the pillow. "Don't worry." But he persists, as his eyes close, he needs to know, "Will you never be able to sleep then? Don't they let you? Don't they ever let you lay down your head?"

When things repeat

the daily pattern. The paper arrives. There is the mail lady, and I wave. I pull the curtains open and there is the day. The night has gone home to Beijing and Manila. I write things down to keep the light from disappearing. A photo with my phone of something Hopper might have painted. The hajib'd fruit sellers. I love downtown in the in-between time changes. I remember the market near the waterfront in Boston at day's end, the ground covered with smashed produce: lettuce, tomatoes, eggplants, fresh-dropped eggs, the spillage of glistening ice, stray dogs lapping up the smell of day-old fish and human labor. Behind the stalls, the fishmongers count their oily cash into the lock box, unlatch their guns. Or the times at dawn in old cities when shops open, pushing up their steel grates, opening for the day. The fresh market vendors setting up tables of blood oranges, ginger, pots of curry, the scent of cinnamon, unhusked corn, great heads of cabbages on carts. The zookeeper tossing huge slabs of meat to the lions. "Roar," he says. The gleaming trumpet bells, cymbals, guitars, and cell phones, motorcycle helmets, a basketball signed by Jordan. Flat screen televisions, old gumball machines and gold chains that are too heavy to put on a neck catching the early light in pawnshop windows. All the common daily wage, the night shift—caregivers, office cleaners, nurses, heads down headed home. I never wanted my poems to be perfectly trimmed. More like a tattered and weather-worn and frayed flag, flying over a country that no longer exists. Like the old grandmother in Haviaras' novel who tells us, "When a tree sings, it's because somebody dies. Or because somebody comes back from the dead." The one who is left (behind) takes the longest path leaving. Where do I begin but in the long after it has happened. This late hour unfolds a fold in the veil. This late hour a fold in the veil unfolds. Is it that every pair of lovers believe in Fate, or do they create it? Too often I face the tragedy or temptation of turning my life into myth when it is really all piss and marrow. To regret the tragedy you have already long traveled. If we have the lamentation of regret, why do we not have a meaning for gret in our language? And if we did, what would it mean? At work the wall clock tocks the time of my steps—this dance I do—what room to check—med to pass. It speaks through walls, shifts, my grandfather's voice speaks of the men he cared for, his round clockface face, coffee black eyebrows, slight clocklike grin, and what was time to him, he who cared and gave, who lifted children from the street and offered them a warm cup. A small plastic cup fills with moonlight streaming through the med room window. If I give this cup of moonlight to the man, he will drink it down. Drink the moon I say, and he giggles, puts the plastic rim to his lip. Blue light of memory streams from his mouth and eyes. Later when he falls to sleep, he will slowly rise, till he is full.

What is the Weight an Old Man Can Carry

At night I bend into the mop, I feel the weight of all my failures pushing my shoulders and I bend, wishing the swishing of the mop could wipe away my grieving. The weight at work an old man can carry. But what if when one is old, we just keep working. It is what I do. I push the weight off my shoulders, as I must lift another man, a man who cannot lift himself, out of a wheelchair and onto a toilet. He helps as best he can. He is not "dead weight." Once he is seated, I turn away as he does what he must do, then lift him slightly when he is done. He pulls up his sweatpants and I wheel him away. He feels so light in the chair, and I remember the poem by Karen Fiser where she imagined wheelchairs that could fly, her wheelchair that could lean down like an elephant. I must lift the man now into bed, and then to sleep he goes, a journey he must take by himself to a place only he can travel. I walk out of the room. What I arrived at work with, it no longer matters. Our lives are not our own. Our lives must be given to another. I think of that photo by Vishniac of the two peasants, the ones in the *shtetl* of my grandfather's people, before the war, hoeing a large field. In the distance are the flowing Carpathian hills, not mountains. A few buildings, a well-made barn. The young man does not wear a hat. The older man wears the Orthodox brim and vest even as he works. Something about his hatless head, the way the young man stands, tells me maybe he is a little slow, and yet his Papa brings him out into the field, side by side they work as the sun crosses the land. They are there, across time, the sun/son pausing as the father turns in mid-stroke. Only after staring at the photo for a long time do I realize the son may be saying something. No, I can hear him now, and he is not speaking, he is whistling. Or is that the wind through the tall grass? The wind that bends and curls along the river

Tiva where the lumbermen move logs. Or the shepherds beyond the frame calling back the sheep. My grandfather, is that you, looking for your cousin? Asking if you can borrow his red bicycle? But there is work to do the uncles say, come with us to the river, bring the long pole to guide the timber. What have I to complain? Even with illness and long labor, we are warm, the bills are mostly paid, the fire each winter is tended. Nothing I carry weighs as much as timber, or the bag of coal the coal man carries to each home. His dark skin darkened more by the dust of ore. But what I carry has a lightness, like a wind-blown hat the farmer is now chasing, as his son the others have named *meshuga* runs whistling, his arms out flapping in a circle like a bird. For such are the slow but sure-footed resemblances of joy. "Menjünk haza, (let us go home,)" the farmer says, and puts his arm around his only child. "Look," he says to him, "in only a day, with only our hands, look at all we have tilled." The man I put into bed is now snoring lightly. I close the door. But as I turn to walk down the long hall, I swear I hear someone whistling.

I'd love to have been a farmer

with a hundred acres, and a silo, a big green tractor with a hound dog named Shiloh to ride shotgun, tending to the rows of corn, or sunflowers, endless fields of sunflowers like I saw in North Dakota, a homemade scarecrow, chickens whose necks we'd spin and snap, a big house that always smells of biscuits and honey, a big boned wife in a bright red flannel shirt, and a half dozen dirty-faced kids I've given old testament names like Elijah, Hagar, Naomi, Tamar, and Jethro, barefoot, scattering up dust as they run playing tag after their chores, but I can barely tend a garden, like the one in our backyard my father-in-law tilled, and my mother-in-law planted, same as every year since I first started it and they took it over. The basil and lettuce has gone to bitter bloom. The unstaked tomatoes bow to the ground where the chipmunks and voles eat them. Deer come and eat the lettuce. I find their hoofprints in the dirt. Or is it something else that comes, stands upright to eat the apples off the tree like a man. My father-in-law and I do not know how they hop the five-foot chain-link fence. My in-laws are good at starting things and abandoning them, lord knows how many half-finished projects they've started over the years. The eavestrough has fallen off. I can't critique them though. The garden is laid out well with wood beds, and we are all getting old. It's hard to sustain much of anything these days. My father-in-law used to be a walking hardware store. He could fix anything. Now I am often reminding him of where he was headed as he stands confused in the middle of the kitchen. My wife and daughters have no interest in a garden, nor a farm. My daughters fly around the block on hover boards and spend as many hours as they can in these virtual online worlds they play with the neighbor kids. Or swim in our aboveground pool. We got it made. This suburban block where three neighbors killed themselves, another two were busted selling drugs, and two more simply vanished when they could no longer make their mortgage payment. I close my eyes and know it must be better milking a cow. After working overtime, my body tells me I am old as dirt. I am old as any levee. The older I get the more I am enamored with the rain, the river, floods, the creek across the highway, the small silver fish that swim, where the boys sit on the bank with homemade fishing lines or digging their hands to catch crayfish or singing frogs. I am older than the sagging porch. I dowse for love with a fallen branch. The dragonflies dive like blue darts through the summer air. The older I get the more enamored I become with the light, like a Rothko painting, the red light, cinnabar and carmine, the hennaed earth along the creek bank. The faded rose sunset, lychee light. The evening's titanium yellow, citrine and dandelion, flooding across the yard's dried grass, itself goldenrod and tan. I am older than the iron gate. A yellowjacket darts above the rotting squash and daffodils. I am obsessed with how ambulance sirens shine brighter in the rain. When we die, I wonder what color the light will be, if there will be light, a kind of blue, a shade of light barely luminescent, the way when the sun sets you can't tell with your eye the exact moment the day became dark. I am old as an old mattress left in a vacant lot. Perhaps we cross over this way? The hours pass so fast, so slow. I am old as Coyote. I turn away and turn back, and my daughters have grown taller. I've lost an inch or so, I've lost a step, a breath. The world turns and turns again. There are no words written in the twilight. I am older than this house, or a hammer, a box of nails made in a factory in China. Old as trade, or envy. Today I saw a pair of tiger-striped butterflies *Papilio glaucus Linnaeus* in the lilac bush outside of the residential facility where I work. I pointed them out to J who lives there and said I've rarely seen that kind this close to the lake. He spent the rest of the day telling everyone, have you seen the tiger-striped swallowtails, do you know how rare they are here? I am old as a darning needle, old as a ball of string. Which reminded me of how we all just want to be part of something rare, special, unique, and often it is a sighting of something alive in this world that can help us make that claim, in this time of extinction, this time going by so fast. I saw two 12-point bucks running along the railroad tracks on my drive to work. I am old as the rust on a Chevy up on blocks by a roadside shack. I am old as an ESSO can, full of rags. I hit the brakes just in time, the bucks paused at the edge of the road, then crossed slow as if daring me to pump the gas. The other day a rafter of turkeys walked across the grounds. I have often wanted to be able to write my name in the steam blowing from a tea kettle but when I stick my finger out, it burns. Once, my daughter said you can't burn your finger on a cloud. We were laying on our backs in the yard's uncut clover amid the drowsy blur of late summer bees. I've often thought that honey is a kind of liquid light, its own sort of yellow. Honey yellow. Honey light. We spread it on the homemade bread we bought at the farmer's market from the Mennonite women, the women dressed in blues, greys, lavender, never in red though I don't think there is any rule against it, heads covered in white, who live on family farms that ring the trailer park where the state troopers just busted up a meth lab, out past the edge of town and have a half dozen children apiece and say *hallo*, and laugh loud when their somber-faced blue-shirted men are not around, and talk to my daughters, stuffing their faces with butter cookies, oohing and ahhing about their scrap quilts stitched with every color—sage and fern, cobalt and carmine, sapphire and chrysanthemum.

Fugue of Four Suicides

The man who lived two houses down killed himself. This was a few years ago. Six months later his son killed himself too, in the same house. Yesterday, two houses down from them another man killed himself. They were all neighbors whose names I did not know, though I used to wave hello to them. The last man who killed himself used to throw fits and scream in his driveway. More than once some neighbor called the cops. I never did. He reminded me too much of the men I take care of with brain injuries. And who doesn't even now and then need to howl at the sun. My neighbor looked a little bit like Van Morrison, with his fat jowls and uncombed hair. With his deep guttural wail. I drink a glass of milk, cold and white as snow. White as the first killing frost. He, we found out after he was dead, had terminal cancer. He'd had enough. The first man who hung himself we heard lost his job and was going to lose his home. His son's story I never found out. The place beside the pond. We aren't the kind of block where people share everything. The son who died was young, in his 20s. To go through life like Patroclus, knowing how it will end. Perhaps that is what these men decided, to know the end of their own story. To write it across the humid air. Will we rise, as the singer Jeff Buckley crescendos, *like an ember in your name?* My daughters mishear me speak of these men and think I am going to die. I tell them yes, but not today. There is a place where all the rivers meet. I tell them don't be stupid, and if I were going to die, you'd go on. Everyone dies eventually, my wife adds. It starts as soon as we are born, our oldest daughter says, and then we are dust. Who knows, I add, maybe not much changes. Maybe we wake up, we wander around those we love. We sit down under a tree and wait. We unpeel a tangerine. We become translucent as the rain. Or maybe we become dust. Is that so bad, I ask my

27

daughters. When you are dead, I suspect, there is nothing like pain. Our oldest daughter ponders, what is it to be nothing. I remind them, nothing disappears. You know, you are stars. Our youngest gleams. Stardust. I wish I had said hello more to my neighbors. I used to see the son up late at night in his second-floor room. Maybe he was listening to music, some song that should have held him. Maybe he played the tambourine? His father hung himself from a ceiling fan. He must have not been fat my oldest daughter smirks. My wife shushes her, but I was thinking the same thing. The house is empty now. The sign for the Sheriff's Sale half-taped to the front door. The same week the last man killed himself my wife went to the hospital for her liver. She said she hadn't been drinking but after she left, we found cans and bottles of alcohol hidden in my daughter's dirty laundry. Do not blame her. The long monotony of living wears one down. I think of the musician Jeff Buckley who, on a whim, dove into the Mississippi. Swept up by the current they found his body miles downstream. Who is to decide the depth marker between suicide and simply careless?

The Dead Who Return as Animals

Like the woman who swore the little dog she adopted was
her dead husband. Just like in all those corny movies, she
said. She said, I know it sounds crazy, but when I brought
him home, she said, the first thing he did was piss on the
cushion of the couch where my husband sat for twenty years
and argued with me. I knew before that though, something
about his eyes. When I said my husband's name, you know
I used to talk to him. Don't you do that? Someone you lost.
David, which should I get? Well this little dog at the shelter
he went crazy. David, I said, David, and him this little black
and white short-legged bulgy-eyed Puggish puppy, running
around in the cage in circles. Some days, he just sits there on
the couch and barks at me. But tenderly. A sort of low huff.
I call him over and put him on my lap and scratch his belly
till he falls asleep. Dogs like this don't live that long, she said.
Just a little more time, she said, he needed to use up what
light was left he took with him. She said, my husband died
before his time. I felt a part of me was torn away. What was
I to do? When we go for walks, I hold the leash loose. He
never chases birds or even seems to see things, turning his
little face to look up at me like I'm the sky. Good David I
say, good. The only time he ever nipped me was when he first
saw the garden out back. It was his garden and I let it go. Oh
he threw a fit when he saw the weeds, the broccoli rabe and
turnip gone to seed, the sunflowers gone to husk. He ran and
carried on *yap yap yap yap yap yap*. Now we tend it together.
Both of us digging. I never liked the feel of dirt before, he
with his new little paws, me with my spade. I used to think I
understood this world when my husband was alive. We went
to work. We did the things we were taught to do. I thought
we were happy. But after he got sick, I cursed God. I cursed
trying to believe there is something more than this world

29

of work and grief. But now look at us, how do you explain this? He's just where he should be. He's come home. Maybe even he wasn't supposed to ever be a person. He seems so happy now. Not the worry he used to carry, never enough money he said. Worry I thought I could never fully erase. A man's life is worry, is what he used to say to me. What did he think a woman's life was? We were happy, but he was always holding something back. But now? I mean maybe somewhere, there's this light right, like how they say, but it doesn't rise right, and there are small furry bodies waiting for us already there, kennels full calling to that light, and what we didn't spend in this life goes inside them, and then they find their people again, that light guides them, or maybe us, the ones they were connected to, the ones still holding on to them like with a leash right? A leash of longing we use to pull them back to us, to fully receive all their unremittent tongue lapping love.

In the Far Orchards After Fall Harvest

I saw a small girl and a woman bending in the orchards along the railroad tracks where I walked with my dog. Her father turned and stared at me as if he might shoot me, then said, "For I was hungry, and you gave me something to eat." And went back to picking frost-damaged apples and putting them in a bag. His wife looked about 45, graying hair and a yellow cotton sundress and boots, and he was in jeans, same as his daughter and two small boys, one wandering, the other sitting on the ground. It was the time just before winter. In the distance, an old model station wagon full of suitcases on the roof. I kept hiking back towards my car, trying not to look back. Today after working third shift, I found a crow's feather like an omen in the driveway when I arrived home. I looked up for its owner but only a few finches, fat robins, some starlings in their murmuration. Once as a child, I flew, like a kite whose string was let free. On a day of a big wind blowing down from Canada I was crossing the street carrying my school bag—I must have been eight or nine—and the big wind lifted me into the air, carried me a half dozen feet. Power lines were falling at the edges of town and trees bowed down as if praying, but I had nothing close to fear when I felt my spine open, and the edge of wings peek-a-boo from my shoulder blades. How often I've returned to the minor miracle of that moment. Sometimes I think I can hear the unfolding minutes the way one can feel a train approach from miles away, vibrating the track. Once I wanted to die and I remembered. If time ebbs and slows, return to Heraclitus in the river. The river moves forwards but sometimes we get lost in a side current, swirl dizzy in a fast eddy. But what if we could simply find a shallow pool along the bank and rest as everything we know and love passes on by us? What great aloneness. There is a tone like *epiphany* that I have long been searching for, but the older I get I wonder of all I missed up to that moment of sudden revelation. Your junkie ex-boyfriend we think is living somewhere in Florida. Remember last decade when he called you on your birthday? He claimed his twins had just died. Those who do not know how to lie, lie extravagantly. When you drink, you are so empty with lies it is like you are handing me a grocery list of items to buy that do not exist: curry pretzel rolls. Jalapeno and maple frozen yogurt. Smoked llama jerky. I'm tired and not even trying to make you look good here. A blank page is never empty. I didn't fall in love with just the good parts of you. Would you have stayed, if we had to pick apples to eat, or steal fruit from an orchard? Perhaps I need the pain you cause me or better art I've learned to give it shape. A cloud passes across the face of the moon. When I was doing rounds last night, I thought someone was dead, and then they coughed.

I used to date a woman after high school whose teacher had been Christa McAuliffe

you know the teacher who was the first private citizen to fly into space, but before she reached it, the Space Shuttle Challenger blew up into infinitesimally tiny pieces. The jokes we told at work that week loading trucks: "What were Christa McAuliffe's last words?" "What's this button for?" I'd like to say I was kind to my girlfriend; her name was Wendy. But she was sobbing hysterically, and I think I might have said, "She was just your teacher, she wasn't your mother." I did not trust collective grief. Maybe it was some instinct about the appropriation of other's suffering. But who are you and I to know about another's suffering? There is something unnamed that weaves us all the way a bee knows to find the flower, or the way the tree has faith that it will rain. In AA they try to teach you not to romanticize your own bad behavior. "What else do I have?" The woman said in session. "Why can't I make it into a story of survival? My story is more than myth." I like to stand and wait for buses I know will not arrive. I am listening to the silence outside the book. We live in a small city on the shore of a lake so large you can see it from space. I hope no thirsty aliens ever find us. I want to make you laugh but I think I am caught in the crevice between laughter and weeping. How startled I was, hiking along the tracks, to find the homeless family gathering rotting apples in the orchard, in late fall. Sometimes when I eat an apple I see that man's gaze piercing into my chest, or his daughter's eyes, green and staring far past me toward something on the horizon. Sometimes I lie to myself and forget that heavy snow erased the world later that week. Nothing here is worth much which means it might be worth more than I can manage. What we witness can be written mythic because at its core, our lives are made of myths we tell and change and tell again and again. What is sacred is as ordinary as hearing an old man cough to tell me he isn't dead. The light that makes the leaves change. Sleeping beside you nothing is familiar and yet what was it worth, watching you in the morning nearly fall, giggling in the opaque light as you balanced on one leg, pulling on your briefs. I have always known I've lived here. How often I return to the morning in a foreign city, in a market where no one speaks our language. I have fallen behind, trying to figure out how much to pay for a bag of blood oranges. I am counting the wrong coins into an old woman's palm. She is moving her other hand *no, nem nem* as if to erase me. Over and over this happens: Our daughter is in a pram cooing, and as you turn and look back at me, a bit of your hair laughs across your face.

Magdalene

There is no stone to roll in this life. Something is bearing on the wind, a woman's wailing. The coins in my wife's jeans jingle as she is getting undressed, and I say, "like the coins of Mary Magdalene." She laughs, even though I've just called her a whore, albeit a quite holy one. Though she is far from a whore, or holy. Perhaps a bit of both, like the rest of us, who are not Mary Magdalene. I wonder about all the men Mary Magdalene slept with before she found Jesus. The moment Jesus ascended, did all their cocks fall off? Burn shaft and balls like instant flaming crucifixions? This has nothing to do with my wife, who was raised Catholic and perhaps believes more than I ever will of something good waiting for us. But Mary was not a prostitute, this is an historical misreading perpetuated in 591 by Pope Gregory I, who mixed up his Marys (let's face it there are a lot of Marys of course including THE Mary, *Madre de Dios*, the blue Mary), with Mary of Bethany, sister of Lazarus. Mary of Bethany is even now lifting her dress. But Mary Magdalene, so named for the fishing village she was born, with the salt sea in her hair, a child whose very first cries were a form of singing, celebrated on the Sunday of the Myrrh. O Mary, there are no coins in your jeans. Witness of the Rolling Stone. Mary, like my wife who is so much more than my wife, but woman, bearer of the unbearable, how much you suffered. You sleep with your feeding tube, not flinching, nearly serene. In the morning you will wake, make our daughters breakfast, prepare to teach them, recite the texts. Drive to your appointments, refuse rest, take your meds. Sleep, wake, teach, contemplate, breathe. Even in death they dismembered Mary's body for holy relics. But she was the original OG Rabbi. There is no translation or human word to say her role, to hear now there is a wordless aria of wind across the lake that names her, scripts her name in rain, the limbs, and lilies, and all our daughters fiercely borne: Bearer of Unbearable Griefs. Witness to the Resurrection, called liar by the other Apostles. How many men have named women liars since? Apophatic angry little sermonic men, who eat alms. Which of them could stand against the mighty voice I hear tonight? Who of them could say they know anything of mercy?

Braille

I am writing about the owl you point out hovering above the drive, like an apparition. You call me to the kitchen window to watch by your side. You hand me a sheet of paper with some scribbles our youngest daughter wrote. I try to read the secret hieroglyphics. What does this say, I ask our daughter. She says, "It is a new language I have invented but it is still teaching me how to read it." Sometimes I suspect the way I feel for you can only be explained by looking at the way a giant green turtle's fins slowly sway through the ocean. For the sound you trail is cerulean, blue ribbons of light. I trace the bruises the IV have left in the shape of Slovakia and Lesotho on your arms. More and more I suspect each day we live is many layered and this life we pass through is just one side of an ever folding and unfolding veil. Or the shape of a letter. The world is a line with many sides we are always writing and shaping each day. The afterlife? An alphabet is still an alphabet even if we cannot read the letters. Getting ready to work first shift today, I am startled how the birds start singing even before they can see the sun rise; it is as if they sense it there, just over the edge of the earth. I forget you are in the hospital, and I go looking for you. I search the children's bedrooms, the downstairs couch, I begin to panic a bit. Remember when your feet first started to have the wounds that wouldn't heal and you had to lay with your leg hanging off the bed, stoned on meds, how you'd leave our bed restless to sleep anywhere, in the living room, in the spare room, even sometimes on the patio's wicker couch, and how our daughters—they were so small— would wake and run downstairs to find you absent and then search the house calling, like a game of hide and seek, pulling me up by the hand, come Dada find Mama, like missing pieces of a puzzle,

and how when they put us back together, you touched grog-
gily like reading Braille your fingers lightly to our faces.

I Have So Little to Offer this World

is something I often say to myself in the worst of times, those days I can barely make it out of bed, but the kids still need their lunches packed for schools, and their mother is in the hospital on dilaudid to ease the pain from her pancreas or her feet. Those days it is the *responsibilities* that get me out of bed, but I go, as they say, through the motions, and not even beautiful motions, not some sort of ballet, or Shaolin, or even yoga, and certainly not like the old people I saw doing tai chi, standing like cranes, or playing harps or lutes in the town square in that city I lived in so long ago it may have been another lifetime, maybe another life. The one I suspect centuries ago I lived and followed Tu Fu, reading back to him his poems before he lit the paper and sent them burning in tiny paper boats or on lotus leaves down the river, the river which courses back and forth in this life so much it is as if it curls back upon itself. And there we are reliving the death of our father, or our daughter's first day of school, or a time I lost my job and those days looking for work when there was none. My daughters are now up and walking through the house completely oblivious to how I feel, which is how it should be: Stop worrying and be a child I constantly say to my autistic daughter who perseverates over everything, who calls herself dumb. "What is dumb," I tell her, "is this world. It doesn't speak and when it does what it says is often cruel. But you and I can say beautiful things—" when she grins, opens her mouth and shouts *"Shiiiiiiiiiit,"* the word she knows we must climb out of already, rising over the rusting yellow school bus that pulls up and opens its door like a great hinged jaw and takes my daughters to the place of rules and numbers. But somewhere today (I know from the paper calendar their mother magnetted to the fridge, they have music) my daughters will be singing, in a room full of children, notes will be taught and there will be arpeggios and off-key sharps, and my wife is on the cellphone to make sure I got them off ok to school, and her voice is a red bird warbling a meandering tune that means she is feeling better and a little high and the doctors say she will be home soon (to be home) is another kind of music: and my old grumpy neighbor walking outside in his jockey shorts and blue robe and black socks to pick up the paper and wave a little wave is another psalm. I glance up at a red-tailed hawk gliding high before it drops in one seamless glissando—a coda for this inane tremulous joy.

Poem Woven with Birds and Grass After Long Hospital Stay

The morning paper opens to a story about a body found in the bay. Snow in moonlight in May, blue as a hospital gown. I take care of a man who seems to forget what he is going to say almost as soon as he is going to say it. What if this is what our lives are, the one before this one receding as soon as this one began?

For decades I have been able to fly in my dreams. What are dreams if not the body's desires? Or are they the desires beyond the body's reach? There is a lamplight I follow down a curved road as if in an old movie, fog-shrouded alleyways and street signs in a language I do not speak but that uses an alphabet I can pronounce. There are certain narratives I refuse to tell.

There is more to being human than what we weep, but what we weep cannot be swept away. Our daughters hover at the edges, hesitant to interrupt your reading, afraid they might hurt you and yet their eyes widen, dark and feral, as if they want to climb back inside you. You with your blue hospital pants you cannot change out of because your legs are too swollen. Home after a week in the hospital. The weeks away add up. A few days home, and then you leave. We rest in each other's presence, coffee, and a plate of blood oranges. I ask for little more these days than to sit beside you as you read. I never thought to ask if you ever wanted a sister. Does time change anything, or it is us who change time? Wait, didn't David Bowie sing that?

A ravishment of sudden rain. *The names of things alive.* Joy: the smell of broth filling a house after a long absence.

When you speak, I hear the names of tall grass swaying in the wind: Little Bluestem blessing the prairie plains, the purple hue of switchgrass, golden Indian grass: *Sorghastrum nutans*. Marrom grass in the sand where we used to nap as our children gathered stones, bouquets of primrose, and wild rye. You are the baker's granddaughter.

When I called you at the hospital, you spoke slow, high on oxy and dilaudid. I see the obscured face of a woman passing on a train. When you speak, I hear cakes rising, I smell the loaves of bread. Your father says, "She seems so angry at me all the time but then I think she is always in pain." What is a father if not one who can take away a daughter's pain?

Warblers, starlings, finches, and thrush. The birds choral above our daughters running with sticks from last night's storm.

Lately, I try to slow down time, the way a photographer slow motions every wing of a hummingbird. I become an alchemist of minutes.

What if we lived on Venus? Each day is 243 Earth days long. I would burn in such a blaze for you if it meant: *stay*.

For too long I was indentured to my grief and didn't see the passing years we have been given. Decalogues of light along the nape of your neck, city streets swept with children, a girl running for the school bus who was once ours, turning to look back.

This week another suicide was found floating along the pier. So instead I will tell you of the white-throated sparrow's trill. I will tell you of the estuary, the terns and gulls. I will tell you of the rusty freighters hauling ore and coal to Michigan, docked in the bay. A cormorant draws a line like a pencil across the eyebrow of the air.

Dusk drapes the willow trees. Or a rusty Ford fender we found washed up on the shore. Your daughter sat behind it honking like a truck. Today, you pruned our youngest daughter's natty hair and bobby-pinned her tresses. You helped with her schoolwork. I write to tell the world, survival is more than love, it is labor: on your worst days home, bone thin, brittle in pain, barely able to move, you pushed my arm away. You stood up.

Eleven

When my wife catches the clock blinking 11:11 she says, "Look the angels are watching." Or is it her dead grandfather, who visits to stroke the hairs on the back of her hand as he did when she was a child? I can feel our dead reach through the veil. I worked with a white woman in a care home on the 3rd shift when she learned on the eleven o'clock news her adult son was dead. They found him in his friend's flat, a pocketful of used fentanyl patches. She opened her mouth to speak but only the dark bird of grief flew from her throat. When every minute of your life becomes the eleventh hour, the dread of waiting? In the long familiar quiet, at his funeral, the mourners moved 1:1. Her son worked at the bakery beside the El. Leaven the grief of this woman pale as an orchid. In the eleventh sentence, I want to ask, what is more unsafe than love? The bread of the body rises. No codeine for the DT hallucinations, hallelujahs at the Baptist church, Venn diagrams fell through the trees outside the Suboxone clinic. Rain crossed the 7-11 parking lot littered with used needles. Pigeons cooed in the cathedral rafters. There are eleven steps to Revelations. The angels herald us at 11:11. At the hospital, there was a nurse named Ekundaya, from Nigeria who would sing softly in Yoruba as she changed my wife's bandages. She nodded at my wife's complaints, the doctor didn't prescribe enough pain meds. Then the nurse said, "Without the pain what would we have to carry?" After Judas died, eleven apostles remained. I wonder if she was one of them.

The Angels are Too Busy Arguing

When they write the history of us it will be a history of absence. The frailties of my wife's body I suspect are due to the brightness of the light she leaks. I have lived with your dying for so many years. What part of you or us is absent? I reach to touch the absent parts, as if one could reach between every drop of rain. Without absence, the rain would be a river. We would be swimming in an ocean. Until we turned to clouds. There is a sky inside my chest that rains and mimics sobbing. The fifth letter of the Hebrew alphabet is *Hey*, which is to say another name for God. *Hey*, what if the Rabbis are wrong, it is not that the Golem does not have a soul, but that it is all soul. So much so that with time it burns everything in its brightness. Was the Rabbi so arrogant he thought he could be given the power of God, to make a life, a being that understands the language of angels? The Golem turns on us eventually because it hears the fear and envy, the jealousy and rage of men, the ark of revenge, all that is outside God, it listens and learns. The dead do not depart. They sway in the wind or lean like in that movie by Wim Wenders. Or the bad remake *City of Angels* with Nicolas Cage as an angel who falls in love with Meg Ryan. But just when he gives up his immortality for love, she dies in a car accident. But it makes sense, right? What is more human than the suffering of the Beloved's absence? The Beloved snatched from our arms? I saw the original movie *Der Himmel über Berlin* when I was young and for days after I would look up—who of us didn't—like an old Italian woman expecting to see the rooftops and parapets high above us covered with strange apparitions watching over us, looking down at our brutal lives. The true shape of love, one could argue, is absence. The depth and breadth of longing. But what of one whose feelings are not the same. The rejected attempts to destroy the object of this obsession. And here perhaps then is some insight: it is not rage or revenge that makes the Golem turn upon its maker, but absence from God. When you are at the hospital, some days I wish they had part-time walk-in mental hospitals—could just check yourself in for the day, get a bunch of valiums, sleep in a white room, then they let you out in the morning no questions asked, a bit stoned, eating daylight. People ask me if I get tired of writing about your illness. I tell them I am writing about the distance one must travel, the weight one must be prepared to bear. When we die, the angel Azrael arrives with one unfathomable suitcase, to fill with all the burdens we did not think that we could carry. Each word I write about us is a history of what the body can or cannot bear.

People Ask Me if I Get Tired of Writing About Your Illness

I confess I am tired love. I watch the dog drink rainwater out of the upturned kiddie pool. This morning there is a murder of crows sitting on a high telephone wire grooming each other and cawing as if telling raunchy jokes. I am writing the history of all the rivers we have crossed. This morning I forgot you were at the hospital. You left when I was half asleep. Grocery shopping, I forget you are not with me, and I stand with the cart waiting for you to catch up. How many years have we glanced back for one another. Once, in Warsaw, the photographer Roman Vishniac saw an old Jewish scholar walking with his head down. Vishniac called out in Yiddish, "How long have you been walking?" The old man said without a pause, "Since the beginning." In the mother tongue *Netivot* means path. We are this path we have not chosen, and I am writing down our days. When you are absent you are never fully absent. The rabbis say God is never absent. I am sure to disagree, but I am writing the way you bend your neck so gracefully to read, the quarter-size port in your abdomen so you can eat. The thinness of your arm I can wrap my hand around. A scarf around your head, you turn to see the finches flutter on the dogwood trees. I am writing how when you sleep, I feel you rise above the bed and fly to me. We sit down at the table on the other side, in the small room on the old street on the hill of that strange city. I can feel your eyes as if you are touching me. You are able to eat the asparagus with butter, the sauteed saffron chicken. We speak in the old tongue. As you talk, the couple next to us falls into a daydream of their childhoods. The waiter hears the lullaby of his dead mother. The cooks begin to sing. All my ancestors spoke impossibly difficult languages. Always your hand in the absence of your hand. O love, I am writing down to let them know you and I go on despite the odds. I remind myself when I am most alone and cannot call your presence, when I feel abandoned, the rabbis say, no matter what evil falls upon this earth, there can never be one hundred percent lack of joy. Now the rain is falling this morning, falling on the roof of the hospital where you are eating broth with your pain pill, the nurses are laughing about something I cannot hear. How their laughter travels down the hall, past those waiting for surgeries, into the pediatric ward where the bald-headed children look up to see balloons. The clown is visiting today. I am writing down the laughter that travels across every human language. The crows are done pruning. Their wet wings glisten like oil. I swear they are all smiling or trying to not show each other they are irritated. Now one gives the other a little shove. *Caw Caw Caw,* and then for no reason they take flight. But I have written this down. They are both flying and still on that wire. The nurses are still laughing. You are still sipping broth. When I reach across to your side of the bed, somehow miraculously, it is warm.

Fugue Written on Unpaid Medical Bills and the Backs of Old Menus

1

In my dream you were not at the hospital, and I became the long legs of a heron walking slowly. Now I remember watching it, realizing it was stalking its prey, eyeing the fish before its long neck and beak suddenly darted almost too fast to see into the water and emerge with a large fish. It was under the highway overpass in the creek where the pair of great blue herons return every year. Our daughter was so young, maybe three, and my son was so tall. We stood watching when our daughter said, with complete awe, the heron was "a dinosaur." Of course, this is precious and near to sentiment except the fact you were not with us because your foot was a pussed mess from a wound that would not heal. I became that heron in a moment and when it spread its enormous wings, rising with that fish in its mouth, I could feel the sun on its ancient shoulders. What is time to a heron—when it walks it's as if it slows down the very fabric of time. I think of the heron watching that fish through the water, how the eye of the bird could see beneath the surface to what was swimming right below the ripples. To find a language to translate—even if momentarily—through the ripples of the veil. Ginsberg said he wanted to do with language what Cezanne did with paint: to capture light on objects. In the other world I dream everything is slightly curved, like looking through a glass globe, or the surface of an eye. There are always hills in the city of my dreams. What is time in a dream when a day can be lived in a few minutes. I fell asleep and you were here, not at the hospital. I woke to the sound of birds on a wire. I put on my scrubs and drove to my shift. Tonight at work with the rain it sounds as if the entire building is breathing.

2
What if the Golem was the Teacher?

The teacher of the language of the birds and fish, the one who can translate the angels. And yet in the novel I'm reading the Golem is reduced to bodyguard, psychopath, psychopathetic/pathic protector. Why? Is it because the Golem is not made directly by God? And who else is not made directly by God? The profound clarity in morning after a night of hard rain outside of a residential facility, or a prison. A sound Johnny Cash might have carried in his chest. Johnny Cash played the steel guitar six string. Johnny Cash played a steel guitar with six strings, he strummed the wind through a prison yard, he strummed a rusty Cadillac down a bayou road, he strummed the dust coming through the windshield on the West Texas highway, he strummed overtime and then night shift every diner waitress of every man punching his clock out for the last time. Where does the great blue heron go next? I wonder this as I drive home from work in the rain listening to Johnny Cash. What is the dark anyways? Something so much more than the absence of light.

3
The Golem

is made of something so much more than the absence of light. Made out of the written word spoken. To make a word, we must make a series of marks. In the place of absence we offer meaning. What is the Ark in every letter? What oceans of light to travel across? What was it that Johnny Cash sang? What a beautiful thought I am thinking concerning a great speckled bird. Johnny Cash who knew the needle's plunge, who sang inside the prison's walls, and knew the prisons we carry inside us. O Johnny, *She is spreading her wings for a journey. She's going to leave by and by. When the trumpet shall sound in the morning, she'll rise and go up in the sky.* Which is maybe where all this is headed? Some sort of gratitude for the wind, the way the trees bow, some gratitude for the light, even when it burns. Some gratitude for the pain, because how could I know the healing without the hurt, or the hurt that never heals? Johnny Cash sang as if the sun itself was the sound of a thousand thousand birds. What is the dark anyways? Something more than the absence of light.

4

A Handful of Paper Cranes Made of Rolling Papers

The one you love nodding out on a beat-up chair. The one you love drunk in a white t-shirt. The little dance you both did when you drank too much, the radio playing some songs from 1964. Johnny Cash singing, *Like a bird on the wire, like a drunk in a midnight choir.* When we danced you did that move like a stoned Mick Jagger, the slow rising of your front leg like a great blue heron. You shook all your tail feathers. You and I are such a small hosanna. A few threads unraveled from the seam.

Alone Among Others

I am a runaway at a bus station near Birmingham. An old white man at the rec center I've taken care of for years, who cannot remember my name, knows his. If someone would have asked me when I was young if one could be this sad and still live, I probably would have said I doubt it. But what did I know about wading through the shallows, step after step, how heavy the feet become? I knew a grief that cuts the wrist, a grief that burns a scar across the chest. Grief is a dive off the cliffs into deep water. The lilac tree that blooms after the long winter. Grief a sharp word. A shard of glass into the heart. At the bus stop on Liberty Ave, I found the two shopping bags full of dismembered plastic statues of saints. Sadness is the shallows one must wade through every day, not trip over the descending last syllable. Waiting for the bus to Bangor, I am the boy punching the vending machine trying to get the chips to fall. Sometimes the most dangerous water to swim in is the shallows. When I am watching over someone sleep, shallow breathing worries me.

The elementary children line up along the stage to sing in their blue shirts and blouses. There is a murmurous sound not quite language from the parents' lips, the snap of flash and light remembrance. My daughter is at the edge of the stage looking as if she is about to leap. I live now in a house of sadness built out of bricks of years, bricks of being alone among others I've learned how much weight the back of a human being can bear. A sadness that never leaves, it weaves a shawl, wraps it around one's shoulders, like the kind any old woman wears, wraps too tight around her neck, some long nights in the chair rocking for her first miscarriage. A sadness steady as a heartbeat? At the supermarket, strangers pass me as I stand amazed the eggplants shine like opals.

A sadness like a stubborn mule that just won't go can carry anything.

Once, Long Ago I Had a Dream of Wild Horses

I was feeling like I could sort of die today, but then I read a poem about Keith Jarett, and I decided to stick around. Who is this bone thin girl counting our change at the corner store to buy a lottery ticket? Keith Jarett who had a stroke and can no longer use his hands. I thought imagine the music in his head he won't be able to play, but then do the hands write the songs, or do the songs simply come from the hands? I often write a poem without my hands. When I taught, I used to give that as an assignment to my students. The cashier at the Citgo Station scratching lottery tickets to cash for strangers, numbers for another kind of life. I once walked past a pawn shop in Budapest that had nothing but doll heads. Dozens staring out at the street. I gasped, then my friend translated as I pointed that it was a "puppet repair shop."

My old man gave me that Keith Jarrett album I loved. I was only a kid, should have been listening to just the Jacksons and Parliaments and Elvis Costello, but I also loved Keith Jarrett, and Jan Gabarek, the slow slur of a saxophone, the way the piano pleaded. I would like to autocorrect parts of my life but leave the written over parts visible. This says something about how I probably put too much value on my mistakes. I am that child carrying an empty metal lunchbox to school. At the Chinese cleaners, the woman takes the man's laundry. There are whole lives that live and die in the breath of steam. Her husband is in the back room on break reading poetry. Is anything we do really a mistake? I suspect we often do more damage consciously than we are willing to admit. The dead child unbends his smashed bike, rides away from the car's fender. It is possible I did not want to die, but the longing for solitude and the longing for death somehow feel the same. In the pool hall today everyone is Chinese, all the exchange students gossiping in two languages about their professors. I have lived with your dying for so many years. What part of you or us is absent? I reach to touch the seam in the veil. In the hospital parking lot the angels were resting their wings: the blue uniformed nurses, smoking on break. I probably work third shift so I can live in solitude, so I can deal with your long death. I watch over people sleeping. I have many jobs but the main reason I am there is to make sure people sleeping do not die. I thought when they were sleeping I would find solitude, but often when they sleep it is as if I can hear their dreams, and my head is full of voices. I write the fragments down on scraps of medical forms. I suspect my memory autocorrects great parts of my life but leaves the written over parts still visible. I suspect the truth is somewhere between the reading of the two. Sometimes a poem is just that, we read it and it takes us back to remembering. Sometimes it takes us forward into the next step. I take a step for Keith Jarret; he leans into the keys. I take a step up the hospital steps. I step toward the sleeping trees. Gabarek lisps a riff. I turn up the radio. I am driving to give my old car to my friend the addict so he can get to work. The notary, this young white man, suspicious of how much less we said the car was worth. Arpeggios rise like ladders to the afterlife. She once told me there were black piano keys that ran up her spine. If my life were a chord, it would be played minor.

3

I Try to Get the Old White Man to Chew his Food

"Slow down." I say, "You'll choke and die." I am fairly sure through his full mouth he says, "Fuck you motherfucker." I walk into a crowded room of caseworkers. I take a step back from the ledge. My coworker, the opioid addict, is calling my cell again for a ride and to borrow money for cigarettes. Suit jacketed and skirted paralegals, eating lunch and gossiping on the courthouse steps. The doctors in their well-starched white coats, the specialists gathered in their little circle outside your room, looking baffled. An old white man in a tank top and cargo shorts, skin like rice paper, nearly translucent in the afternoon light, offers his arm to a woman in halter top, breasts unbraed and sagging to her belly, as they step to cross at the crosswalk. They walk or should I say shuffle so slow the pedestrian signal changes. I glide beside them, as they are bent-headed and unaware. I spread my arms to the oncoming traffic, wave cars and buses around them and on to the places of their separate lives. Keith Jarrett understood the rain, he understood the way dark is a color not a shade, the way blue and grey are kinds of light. He understood the keys and pedal are the body and the body is a kind of bruise. In the cafeteria at the VA, the man I caretake sees his old comrade from the Vietnam war, "Here," he says, "Here, Jack, you, you take my applesauce."

Beautiful hatted Black women spilling out of the Baptist Church, children running around their legs, as I drive home from work on Sunday. After everyone is gone inside someone is still playing the organ. Is everything we witness, every minute that unfolds, a hallelujah, or an amen? There is a chorus of grackles in the trees. In the diner, I watched the red-haired waitress pour the coffee, scribble orders, smoke on break. The place was full of truckers, off I-80. I ate my apple pie with a fork and knife. The waitress was talking on a cell phone to someone about her man and bail. She didn't have a ring. I told her I missed my daughters, and she didn't mention any kids. She was old as me, old enough to be someone's grandmother. All around me were Black and white men in trucker hats and hardly anyone was talking. Staring into their palms. Beneath the chatter of the news and weather I could hear them breathing. At 2 AM, I went to check a man's O2 levels and on the way the ghost said, "Hey." I was rushing and nearly forgot to check on someone else, so I slowed down, I took my time. I watched a man's chest fall and rise. I turned down his stereo. I walked to the next room. Sometimes the dead are just there to say, "Hey, don't forget to open this door."

Poem Made of Fragments Written on Various Pieces of Paper—Napkins, Social Work Papers, Med Order Forms, the Back of Med Supply Receipts, Gas Receipts, and Some after Waking from Dreams

I did not kill myself today. It was a Tuesday. And since you are reading this, neither did you. Neither of us were sent to war or had to hide in the basement. No one was standing under the streetlight at 3 AM. I tend to walk with my hood up, my head down. I tend to take my hood off if I see a cop. I tend to look away from bridges. The day the crocuses arrived I feel a part of me glanced up at the cardinal and flew away. Camus wrote, the moment that Sisyphus lets go of the stone, there is a moment he is free. But I say why doesn't he sit down? Why doesn't he refuse to go on? Is there not a Union in the afterlife? No wonder when we die, they used to say, "He punched his clock." During the Balkan wars, who was the cellist—I googled it!—Vedran Smailovic, who brought a chair to the square in Sarajevo, sat down during the siege, and played *Adagio in G Minor*. Death prefers the minor keys. Vedran Smailovic is still alive. He is still playing in concert halls, but behind the veil he is forever playing in the square as the snipers look into their sights. And here is the ghost girl running through the halls again. Where has she come from? There are moments it seems I cannot even spell my name. As if I myself have been disappeared. Then I return. Sean, I write on the form that says I watched over humans tonight, and no one died. Is everything I write about your absence? How it hovers above you when you bend your head to read. When I was a boy, I used to love to take apart old radios. Not to see how they worked but to see how they looked like a miniature city, with tiny streets, skyscrapers of tubes, bodegas of fuses. Once, years ago, I walked far out onto the ice, and when I was out far enough that the world was only sky and clouds and frozen lake, I sat down. There is no anniversary for this day. I drive past the abandoned farmhouses. I am the sadness of horses standing in the rain. I learned to love you the way one learns to love the emptiness of winter fields. I tried to put you away in a drawer full of lost things. I found you in the coffee grounds this morning. And in this way, the voices drift, labyrinthine. An emptiness like a cathedral in my chest. I ramble along the tracks, a bit wary, a bit weary, headed towards nowhere I can name. There is nothing here to translate, sentence by sentence on this earth we are bandaged or bound to grieve. I lay down in the park, drowsy in the afternoon light. I begin to disappear. Leaving behind the weight I've carried. If you were to try and find me, all you would see in the grass is the hollow my body made.

No, I Will Not Go in the Empty Room, Because If I Go into the Empty Room, the Room I Was in Will Become Empty

The Archduke Ferdinand was assassinated by a Serb, but not Franz Ferdinand the Scottish band who transformed alternative rock in the mid-2000s, when we Americans made lots of dead with our bombs and our wars, but Franz Ferdinand the band was from Scotland, not the Austro-Hungarian empire. Of course Scotland also has soldiers killing for the archaic Queen of England, marching with their obscene kilts. All so removed from the Archduke who was long dead, shot in Sarajevo only a couple years after my great-grandmother boarded the George Washington, at the port of Bremen, and sailed to New York in 1912. The Archduke was the last ruler she lived under before sailing away with her cousin Rose for America. She a black-haired brown-eyed Hungarian Jewish woman. Hair black as our Bosnian neighbors, the grandmother who escaped Sarajevo. They flew on a jet. This America is one of departures, and luck. For what if my great-grandmother had never boarded that ship? Before the Great War? When the soldiers all across Europe dug their trenches, she was already ensconced in Yonkers. And it was the Serbs who murdered my Bosnian neighbor's sister, brothers, cousins. The Serbs who shot the Archduke. And it was a Serb who taught me poetry, and who I once fell in love with. In order to write the poems I wish to write, I must live longer than I suspect I will. So I must write as if I am already dead.

Perhaps we have premonitions, not to change the future, but to prepare us for what will arrive. For love is a leaving, and an arrival. The departure of the dead. And what ground is not blessed by the dead if you travel through a century or two? You must ask, am I the martyred, or the murderer? How many of us travel with a bit of blood of both? My great-grandmother died of influenza. Her husband told her to brush it off. Ignored she got worse. My old cousin says he was "a bastard of a man." Weeks later the windows were covered with black cloth. My great-grandfather married her cousin. My grandfather, once he was a grown man, never talked much about his father. When my grandfather was dying, his dead mother came to the room and stroked his forehead. He spoke to her as clear as if he could see right through my body. For my people call their dead before we arrive. Somewhere the table is already set. I think of this when I place the spoon beside the bowl. How the old will lift the spoon and stare at their face in the curved reflection as if to say who is this stranger? I often think the white space on the page is like the frozen lake, a field of snow, a room without corners. With each keystroke we leave our strange footprints to be followed to the horizon line. What is there beyond the curve of the earth, which is very much like reading a sentence. Not even a word is fixed. A fragile biology of letters held together by a skein of sense. Only the thin skin of meaning. Which is why I love alphabets I cannot read. They are shapes like a person. For a person you can never fully know. Which to me like love always feels more tragic at the beginning because the beginning has the feeling of the end already in the first gestures. Perhaps that is why we use in our language the infinitive *to fall*. Like autumn, when the trees' leaves are fullest red, they have already long turned to bare branches. What I want but cannot ever hold is the ephemerality of every falling leaf as it writes a new sentence in an ancient alphabet across the autumn air.

Eating Cartoons

There were no sirens in the distance, no sound, not even the El. The steel blue that is Donald Duck's hat. Can we drink his hat? Can we drink the dark? What will it taste like? It was then I knew I was in a dream. I was chewing on a piece of a cartoon like it was a smoked turkey leg. I woke up hungry to write this down. I remembered my daughter had woken me up out of sleep. On the nights I work third shift she climbs into bed when she wakes to sleep with her mother. But tonight our daughter returns to bed uncomforted. I want to tell you this poem isn't about my daughter, or her mother, or work, or worrying about our unpaid bills. It isn't about insomnia or the sound of traffic heading off for first shift. It is only about how wonderful it would be if we could eat cartoons. Thin sheets we'd hang on fire escapes between huge tenements like in Hong Kong or Donkey Kong, dry them like hemp, we'd cut and fold to eulogize the living, and let them go through our projector eyes. Can you see them reflecting in my pupils, the television my mother turned on for me as she bent over the big books to study. She has placed a sheet of cartoons in the oven to bake. I can smell the falling anvils are burning. She brought me a bowl of pratfalls. A plate of TNT. She was a young radical law student, then in a city that no longer exists, in another century. I eat the bread of Wile E. Coyote falling off the cliff. A cartoon of cold milk I'd pour like static. Down our open throats they'd go like singing. Each Saturday morning, I tell my disbelieving daughters, was the only time they showed cartoons. I'd sit for hours watching on a 19-inch tv that weighed as much as me, rabbit ears bent to the signal (what are rabbit ears?). I stand to show them on one leg, like some great addled ostrich who has lost its egg, and they are laughing, spitting milk, as I teeter and make the sound of electromagnetic radiation, (the

sound they told us in school is the sound of the universe un-
folding, the sound of time itself), in a rented house long torn
down, in another century. I wish I had turned more from the
wise guy talking rabbit, to witness my young mother beside
her enormous book pile, in her serene silence, head bent as
she turned the pages of tiny words.

Death Letter #3

I woke to imagine a world that had lighter gravity, where things float in the air as if in water. Entire groves of white birch trees hung like clouds, trailing their black roots like tentacles that caught the rain. Beds of brilliant blue and red and yellow flowers, nasturtiums, and marigolds, grew just higher than head's length as the air above my head was full of a brilliant buzzing. Herds of wild Appaloosa roamed unfettered, and yet I could not rise, so full of something weighing me down I could not let go. And then I saw the children, whole platoons of them, true Cherubim, giggling as they rushed by as if an invisible river. It was the morning of the eclipse I dreamed this; the world woke to a ring of fire. I feel myself die a little more each day, time pushing us forward in the contrapuntal two-step we do, each year passing the anniversary of our own passing without knowing. This is nothing new or even original, but lately I can feel it more, feel time slipping, like a substance, like wind or water, or maybe something both physical and ethereal, like hunger. And you have lost so many pieces of yourself the doctors have removed. First was your toe, then your teeth, your gallbladder, and your appendix. Your poor pancreas holding on for "dear life." I never really thought of the epistolary nature of the phrase "for dear life," as if one is writing a letter to life itself. Dear Life, we begin and tell our story. All day the tulip tree has been trying to tell me my grandfather is calling. What is the secret name of the wind? Or should this be what is the secret name of a cloud? I cannot hear the grass today for the lilies' incessant weeping. On the news, some feel-good story from the space station, and I ask am I lucky or cursed to live in a time when machines and human beings look DOWN at the sky. An emptiness that is not holy, as if one is exiled across a vast water, or veil. The yard is littered with the long-unplayed toys of my children. Chesed: "The divine emanation of kindness and mercy." Who of us is not Abraham entrusted with the garden of Eden? Without you, my wife, how would I have learned of mercy? Without you, what would I have known of mercy? Our daughter's skin has the scent of gardenias from the garden. When a thousand miles away, my friend's aunt died, she said she woke up screaming. How did you know, we asked? All the women in her family smell roses at the moment one of them dies. The caregivers know death has a scent, like slightly rotting wet petals in a rain-filled ditch. Decades ago I worked in a factory that smelled like death and flowers. It made things for weddings. There was an entire line of women, aged from eighteen to their sixties, who twisted wedding garlands. "Less talking," shouted their supervisor, though she was probably the loudest, swearing and laughing all shift. They never missed quota. They worked in white smocks buttoned to below their neckline and white hairnets. Giant vents blew a breeze in summer that rustled everywhere. The white woman in her fifties, Janet, who ran the line, all thin bones and scolds, and yet they loved her. She was the toughest, tannest thing I'd ever seen. Her hands hard-knuckled as brass. There was a room where a man wore a mask as they mixed chemicals in a giant vat to make potpourri. I worked the dock loading trucks. To this day I swear there was nothing more like freedom than witnessing those women spill out on break to the parking lot and pull off their white hair nets and let down their thin or voluminous hair for a time, shaking their heads, sharing lighters, borrowing cigarettes, gossiping in the parking lot. This was over thirty-five years ago. The factory is long closed but still every time I pass some wedding shop or catch the smell of potpourri, I think of those women I worked beside, the light they carried inside them, and I know some of them are gone. But what I've come to understand is what we've joyed or suffered, loved or sang, never fully vanishes. It lives on inside us like the dead. And what is more, I've learned that what we are is so much more than just witnesses for this labor. We are the mercies we have been given, and the mercies we have made.

Biscuits

Sometimes when I look at the sky I see the clouds become figures seated at a big table. Look, my mother-in-law says, those clouds look like the Last Supper. But it is more like the last brunch, on any Sunday not Mother's Day, at the Polish Falcons social club, and all the bushas gossiping about so and so's cousin and so and so just died, and did you hear her granddaughter married a doctor, or so and so's son is out of rehab etc. Those women who worked in machine shops for decades, side by side, like my mother-in-law who worked twelve-hour shifts, six days a week, with a foul-mouthed foreman who tormented her, until my mother-in-law just took the buy-out and retired at 62, spit at the feet of the old bitch on her last day, in front of the molding machine she gave forty years—retired to let her bitterness ease with each passing win at bingo. Now she laughs easy, goes out with her girlfriends, reads her romance novels and every Stephen King, does no housework—"Remember I worked forty years in a shop. I've done my time." Loses days due to her migraines, her scoliosis, her slipped disk, offers up her inappropriate jokes learned on the shop floor, those tough women, with their fulcrums and their wrenches. She never learned to drive, her old shopmate picks her up and off they go to the social clubs, to buy the pull tabs and split the winnings, and the losses, sneak a vodka before she comes home, and half listen uh huh and um hum to her husband drone on and on about his model trains, or how somebody visited the neighbors this afternoon. Today I watch her out in the garden. She doesn't really like to plant or dig, but I see her look up a lot—what is she staring at? Oh the clouds, that big table of bushas, daughters of immigrants, up there, blowing on the big wind over the big lake, back to the motherland, and the great fields of wheat, clouds you know—

the off-white billowy kind she tells me, "look like a cooking sheet of just-baked butter milk biscuits."

Poem as Pedagogy or Prose Poem that Includes Prompts for the Reader

I have no memories that are not partly fiction. Ask me to tell you a memory and what I say is apt to change by the telling. Every time we tell a memory we rewrite it a little more. Even as I write this, what I was going to tell is starting to form and shift. I was going to tell. But memories can be fixed too, fictionalized by objects, photos, film. I often wonder if my early memories of being a child in Brooklyn are not simply the recall, the memory, of watching those Super 8 films my grandfather took. In my mind, I always seem to be seen in 3rd person.

Prompt #1: Write a one sentence scene of yourself as a child. Then write a tight descriptive paragraph to establish narrative authority before it becomes fragmented, such as ___. End on image such as: my dead grandpa.

What are the dead made of, if not memory? *Remember* is such a static word (still word?) without the infinitive to. Although it can be heard as declarative, a kind of order: *remember* as in the imperative tense. To remember. When does remember become a form of righteousness? Remember me, the dead say. We say the shape of a memory but do memories have shape? What is the shape of every passing day but the rooms and roads we pass through?

Prompt #2: Offer a sequence of metaphors for memory.

Something about the leaves. And what do our bodies recall? Or recant? Something about the moon. The absence of my grandmother's eyes I could not enter. Perhaps our bodies are mostly memory (machines)? I remember when I was a boy in school, I was taught to memorize a poem by adding body gestures. Most of what I know I think lives inside my hands. My grandfather once told me, some men start to die when they cannot work with their hands. To make a thing and hold it shining. How confused the professors looked when they asked how I write my poems. I said, without sarcasm, I wrote poems with my fingers.

Prompt #3: Make a poem without using your hands.

But how will it be remembered? At this point in my life I fear I have forgotten more than I can recall. Perhaps it is always this way? We filter out the day. *Remember* means literally to rejoin the group. Who is pressing the accordion keys in my chest? My friend Dave says he has Irish Alzheimer's. He only remembers the grudges. He worked 30 years in the diesel-engine factory before he retired. Why can't I let the memories go? Remembrance as trauma. To recall only the grudges, the pain, the abuse. To erase the present. Where do we travel but in time?

Prompt #4: Write a poem that takes place in a few seconds.

Who says to remember is to honor God? Who says to forget is a gift God in his mercy has granted? The mercy of forgetting so we may go on. To let go, as the leaf lets go of the tree and falls it writes out the secret name. All I want to remember are the simplest things, the moments without language I want to write, the way the wind brushes the hair across the forehead of my four-year old daughter. I want to forget the times I was curt, the times I did not listen. The time I heard the words but not the tone. The tone of a day, as in music, rich and Baroque, slowly unfolding, adagio, or even minor chorded in the rain. How my daughter and I ran dancing in the downpour's timpani. The cello of remembrance bows across the afternoon light. My mother-in-law is staring out at the street, the long look of long melancholy. "What are you thinking I ask her?" She just answers, "Humph," the way I'd catch my own mother. Sensory. Inhale the scent of the madeleine, and Proust was lost in revery. Saute onions or bake a cake. Breathe in. What do you see? The smell of a garage, oil on a man's hands? A certain lavender scent of perfume? The day the cherry blossoms bloom? What does it all mean? What returns to you? For memory is made of scent. It begins with our noses; they track the scent of time. Procedural. To tell you how to do something.

Prompt #5: Write a paragraph that explains how to do something simple which you do every day.

What has to happen in language to make it more than an instruction manual? To do a thing is to know it. We must remember the steps. What are the steps to erase sorrow? What are the steps to write forgiveness? I have a story to tell but I worry it isn't true. I'm not sure I write poems anymore as the attempt to make a sentence. Something about water. A sentence is a sort of seam between this world and the next. Something about the sea. In Kabbalah, the Rabbis say there is a sequence of letters that spell out the secret name of God. My great uncle and his violin. A failed attempt to remember a place of air and light. And there is my long-dead cousin, rushing to work at the timber mill, carrying his prayer rug and an awl. For the marrow of this life is dirt and piss and shit. Something about an outhouse. The green-headed horse-flies. The plastics factory where my mother-in-law worked was another kind of hell. Which is to say she never talks of the forty years she worked twelve-hour shifts.

Prompt #6: Write a memory without commentary.

Down along the 12th Street tracks, the cathedral-like enclosure of the steel plant, with its dome of broken glass. Children chasing pigeons along the train tracks. Noon, there was no one on the platform waiting. For recollection is more like the long shadows of evening. My wife's dream of pistachios. The palindrome of time. To tell a story is to emit light. My wife woke up at night and spoke in her dream, "You are hiding from me." I said, "I am right here." She said, "Your heart, you never kept your heart out in the open." Then she rolled back to sleep.

Prompt #7: Write an essay where your heart is out in the open.

Prompt #8: Write a poem where your heart is hiding.

Who will find it? What is the role of the reader? As we've discussed, time spelled backwards is emit?

Now rewrite your poem backwards. Begin with the end. It matters who asks you to tell you your memory. Tell it to your coworkers. Tell it to your widowed grandmother. What is true is what we tell as best we can, for the body will remember. The body is a letter we are always writing.

4

Story Told at Lunch by a Friend whose Lover had Recently Left Her

My friend Kiko told me today of the dead boy who lived near the edge of the woods in her village. Everyone said he died in the last tsunami. He did not hear the warning siren, they say. He could not escape the water fast enough and was trapped. Some say he was a street child, who never paid attention anyways. But I say that cannot be true, she said. A boy who lives on the street would have senses and street smarts. He would know to hear the siren. He would know to follow the flocks of birds to high ground before the wave arrived, she said. No, he was a boy who had been left behind, a boy abandoned by the people who were supposed to love and watch out for him. I think this, she said, though no mother claims him, though many claim other boys. They too are a kind of dead, these leaving mothers. These weeping mothers no better than orchids. I think of the boy's parents. Maybe they were dead already. Maybe he was an orphan being raised by his grandmother, his grandmother who was deaf, and could not hear the sirens. *Baabaa, Baabaa,* he would say, pulling on her blouse. Suddenly all was shadow.

Kiko took a sip of her tea and stared out the window. It was a rainy day and the yellow of passing taxis looked brighter in the falling rain. She said the boy would come and beg for a bun from the street vendors who felt pity. They would give him one, but the boy would never eat it, he would sit and hold it in his two small hands. He would lift it to his nose to breathe in the sweet scent, and sometimes he would smile with his mouth closed. It seems he could not open his mouth to eat or respond to questions. The dead, they say, are driven by the desires and needs of this world. They want to eat; they need our love. But they cannot swallow or say the words they carry within them. All the words they wished had been said or said to them when they were alive. There is no other side for the dead. Do you think he chose to stay among the living, I asked her. She stared again out at the street and the rain.

Who knows, she said, why anyone chooses to stay or leave? Who knows why one dies when they do or another lives? I looked down at her small hands, holding the cup of tea, the steam rising, molecules that were once water now turning to air, and I thought of them rising out of this tea house, out of this room in our lives, escaping up into the sky where they would become clouds, that would one day rain, that would fall into a well, where an old woman would ask a boy to pull up the bucket for her, and in a room of thin walls, she would fill the kettle with that good well water, put it on the blue ring of fire, and when it was ready it would boil and whistle. She would pour the tea into a cup and he would hold it, the boy breathing in the sweetness of it, the steaming sweetness of this good earth, before it passes.

Once Was

my cousin, *balleboste,* good homemaker, there standing at the right edge of the frame, in a basement flat in Warsaw, how she folds her hands so formal, held across her belly for the photo. In the basement kitchen she might say if asked, *altz if gud,* all is good, perhaps a bit sardonic. The wall collaged with propaganda and theater posters wheat-pasted as if to patch a hole to keep out the cold that seeps through the ragged wall. It must be cold, as even inside she is wearing a thick coat with two big wooden buttons, and a scarf, bowed low on her neck, a slight touch of style, one that says I am more than wife or mother. I am urban and not Orthodox. A secretary in a factory. Her head not scarved. On the other side of the frame is a tall white pot of boiled potatoes. Hung from the low ceiling is a net sack of onions. At least here no one is yet hungry. On the stove, a kind of fire pit on blocks, a tea kettle, and a frying pan. Hung on the wall is a large paint-chipped ladle for soup. But nothing is cooking yet today, and there I see at the side of the photo what looks like a wool carrier with two rope handles. Yes it is a *Moshe bateivah!,* A hand-woven Moses basket! But inside, is cradled only a doll made of *shotf shmate,* that is cloth rags precisely tied and twisted into a tiny human figure. And where is the child? I believe it has not yet arrived. It is still kicking forever beneath her folded hands.

Death Letter #1

"You do not believe in God, I said to myself, so why do you believe in bad luck?"

Charles Simic

or death? You don't believe in God, but you believe in death, say he was here last night again, the tall dark shadow standing over my side of the bed, on the wall, by the bookcase. I wonder if he was just here to borrow something to read. Anne Sexton's Collected, or that last book of Lorca. If death speaks any human language, I suspect it is Spanish. *Dia de los Muertos.* But he loves silence most of all. Perhaps you have invited him these years, my wife says. I'd never thought of that, the same way I never thought that when we returned from another life, my wife says, we might bring all the regrets and resentments we had from that previous life. Well, that's kind of a downer, I say. I thought those would be left in the dust. I thought we might return clean. I thought I would be free of any baggage. Of course Irish Alzheimer's means: you forget everything but the grudges. I wonder if death ever makes noise, say when Alejandra Pisnarik reached for the bottle of pills? "All night I see something lurch toward my looking, something humid, contrived of silence launching the sound of someone sobbing." I like to read what I write to him; I tell my wife. He likes best the pauses between the words. He is lonely I think, standing there, little more than a shadow, and yet his shape is the hand we must all hold, princes and paupers, prostitutes and presidents. I have never run from you, I say. But she is not yet yours. I cannot play chess, or the lyre. I will not climb through the black door in the ceiling. Sit down I say. They say never invite death in, but death is invited in the day we are born. You have the best hoodies, I tell him. I always preferred you as the ferryman, rather than with that scythe. Though you could be my ancestor, slicing the Carpathian wheat. I know you spent too long there, along those mountains, so much there is a permanent shadow that crosses the river Livia, dark shadows like fish in the Danube. A shadow without breath. You pole into the deepest water but here you have a walking stick. An old branch like an old man's arm. Or is that you? I thought I saw you in the chair beneath the oak tree, my grandfather was across the yard, whistling under the tulip tree. I met you in a dream I had of endless fields of sunflowers. I was me and not me. My name was different and so was yours. I saw you holding the reins in the wagon of the dead. Outside the dead child's room at the hospital I saw you were a little girl, holding a flower, holding a balloon. Holding the red ball out with straight arms. Why does my neighbor who killed himself stand by the side of the highway? He stands so straight he could not be human. Along the bend, I slowed my car to see his faceless face. Or was that you? Are all our dead a little piece of you? I do not think it is you who weaves the veil. The thin place at work where the dead caregiver crosses to tell me to check the rooms. The crows wear their black suits, their formal dress, to honor the dead. One crow who moved too slow is dead at the foot of the drive, cut with cat's claw and fangs. His comrades caw and jostle, wobble and push, lined up on the line, they are like the drunken uncles, highly inappropriate in their habit, always saying a bad joke just as the rabbi is about to give the blessing. Every letter in our alphabet makes meaning with a black line. But no line in a letter is simply black. There are many worlds beyond this one, I dream death says. He is reading a Hollywood magazine. He knows all the latest gossip. The childhood stars about to overdose, crash and burn. He knows the steps to all the dances, he sends that shadow into the air as the ballet dancer leaps, the Polka's mad Mazurka, the breath he breaths into the accordion. A few dark petals swirl around my feet on the back porch. My dead grandfather asleep beneath the tulip tree. I didn't know the dead could wake and sleep. Do they dream? In the flamenco dancer's feet and fingers, he gives the rhythm. The dead flower's blossoms were dead long before it died. And time ceases in ¾ time. And time ceases in ¾ time, the waltz we do, spinning like a planet around a sun. A solar system. A galaxy. And between everything is the silence and the singing dark we cannot hear, the cosmic rays plucking like piano strings. It's my blood I hear tonight as my wife and daughters sleep. I am waiting to ask him a few things, a story of a boy lost in a tsunami, of a child crossing a border. Of a woman long widowed who sews and psalms. Hope, what is hope to him? I do not believe he knows the end for sure before it arrives. The day he reaches for my hand, I will ask for one small last favor. I will unroll the giant scroll of paper I have saved under our bed. I will give him my pen. We will write our last poem together. The first line and the last are his to rhyme.

Poem that Starts with a Photo of a Woman Faraway Walking through the Carpathian Hills

Like the angels, the Rabbi says, who fly so fast and often between this world and the next, they sometimes forget whether they are coming or going. Between the snow-covered fields dictated by absence, the dark figure of the woman on the long well-trudged path one hundred years ago. She could be my great aunt, or a stranger sent to gather wood. It is hard to tell if she is leaving, or is she arriving? She is just a smudge, a dark note of history at the foothills of the mountains. We wake up each day, which is to say this is a simple miracle. Even if one cannot get out of bed? Even with suffering. Even if one cannot walk far away. The woman will arrive to pull a bedspread up at the edge of the fire. My daughter surprised me when she said, "We are always driving to a door. The house, the store." I said, "What about the beach?" She said, "The lake is a door. So is the sky. Or maybe instead it opens like a book?

Look—" And she stuck her finger to the window. "I am opening the book of the sky. I am writing letters. I am reading." I nearly drove off the road.

Even if there is only loss, slowly we can tell, sorrow cannot erase it all, or else it was not love. Say this to those who suffer, or those who do not. Jean Valentine wrote, "this close to God, this close to you." But there is suffering and there is pain. Pain is the enemy. The woman's feet in the photo are cold. This I know, no one can walk that long and not feel cold. This is all that matters to me, that she is headed to a well-kept fire, that she has kindling. "What about being alone," my daughter asks. I hadn't considered that. "Where are her children?" "Maybe," I say, "she is very old." My daughter asks,

"Who will take care of her then?" "She takes care of herself," I say. "This is what it means to grow old." "I thought to grow old," she says, "was someone needs to take care of you?" I say, "Not right away." All of these are wishes and suppositions which I think, perhaps, are things of wanting rather than to gift. Today I woke up. My wife is fighting hard to remain out of the hospital this week. She only has a handful of pills to help. She is tougher and more beautiful than I can ever manage to get her to believe. Every day her fractures reveal light that shines from her body's vessel. I watch her read and realize that silence is not the opposite of music, but what lets us hear the music beneath our skin. The children are fed and on their machines. Our youngest humming like a humming-bird, she flutters back and forth to show us her electronic drawing. I worked a long shift the night before and no one was ill. One woman did not know the difference between day and night and kept waking up to play cards. I told her it was too late to play cards. She said, "What am I supposed to do!" When the body's own understanding betrays us, when time slows down, we reach out for another. "Here, I will walk you to your room," I said. I adjusted her air conditioner. I said, "It is so hot. No wonder you could not sleep, you had the heat on." She said, "I am always cold when I travel." I turned amused. "And where are you going?" I asked. "Home," she said. How hard to hold it in. I turned and arranged a few things for her, a hairbrush, put her toothbrush back in the bathroom, made sure she hadn't run out of toilet paper as bad days she will forget to mention. She wanted to show me each and every picture of the photos of her families, but I had work to do, paperwork, filing for the other shifts, and others sleeping to check. Still, there was a kind of absence she needed fixed. I stayed as she flipped the well-thumbed photos, this one is her son, now grown she remembers he is no longer a baby, but, "He is still my baby, his father didn't do anything, he was nothing but a sperm donor, I raised him, I raised them all, by myself, doesn't that make me a good person, aren't I a good mother, now look this is his baby, now I am a Baba, I have to be strong. I was hit by a drunk driver, but I keep going, seven years I worked as a bartender." She kept talking, a long string she said as much to herself as me, over and over. "This is Frankie Sue Wilson, my best friend, she had eleven brothers, who names a girl Frankie, she was such a tom boy. I was a tomboy. Who wants to play with Barbies: I loved football, we'd chase each other around a tree, her brother was my best friend, but he killed himself, he was a cop." I've heard variations of these loops she says everyday over and over for years, and yet she says them as if to anyone to fill the absence, to make something between herself and others. But what are we each carrying into the night? What load so one cannot rest? What I tell her begins with a letter. What she says back to me begins with a letter. She is just a woman, a just woman, in an institution who cannot sleep. A woman whose children and mother rarely come to visit her. The mercy of time is she no longer feels time. Every day she does not sleep is a miracle. Every day she wakes is a miracle. She can be angry and temperamental, brittle as the glass figurines she keeps locked in a case, a collection from her childhood we have somehow kept her from shattering through the years. She pulled out another large pile of photos from a box. Some of the photos of her children are black and white, well-shot and framed. There is a gray and gritty beauty to them, a shine like gray glass. One of her sons, maybe 15 years old, in a white t-shirt, marine-cut short hair, behind him it is dark, turning back to look at her in the flash, not able to tell is he walking towards or away. A boy who was never hungry, the two jobs his mother worked, bartender and at the bakery. This woman who worked all night before her brain injury. No wonder she can't sleep! "Who took this one?" I asked her.

Surprised to think in all the years I've cared for her I failed to ask that basic question. She paused, I've tripped her up. The first silence in long minutes. The long litany on pause. I felt something enter or leave the room. She nearly jumped up. Pressed the photo to her mouth, shouted, "I did. I took it. I did."

Hasidim, Brooklyn Light

Some black-bearded young men on cell phones, others old with white tinged beards down to their waists, mothers with long black dresses pushing prams and chuckling Yiddish lullabies. The teenage girls come running, their tight jeans rolled above the knee beneath their long plain dresses—in the subway station, out of the eye of their parents, they lift their hems, unsheathe themselves—the transformation into bad—each doing the other's makeup—blue eyeliner, deep red lipstick, and hair sprayed high, prayer books stuck in big purses with flats exchanged for blue and glitter fat hip hop soles. These Hasidim girls become all bassline, swaying and pointing, half-shifted, navel-pierced, vowels deep as Brooklyn. How did that one hide the tattoo of a bird on her calf? Whose grandmother too wears tattoos? Suit worn to threads, sitting baggy on the bench, nearly nodding into his chest, one old man moves his lips as if praying. And I am reminded how one sect says, there is never one hundred percent lack of joy—cantors rising on cumulus clouds, tangerine sound of ice cream truck bell lilt-lilting-feet run-running across Eastern Parkway, the children—all yarmulkes and braids, never one hundred percent lack of joy. Can there be one hundred percent joy? Dim the day goes, sundown, on the Sabbath, late April. Five thousand years the letters become sounds. The cherry blossoms voweling *yes yes yes*.

My eleven-year-old daughter asks for a pill

to sleep, she's already had two melatonin. If I was working tonight she could crawl into bed with her mother, but I will be up all night and her mother is already asleep with our youngest, so I say take two, or three, or you could just try to dream, try to talk to yourself, tell yourself the most boring story, about a little house. She says "A little house where I can watch the paint dry." I hear her giggling in her room, nowhere near sleep. Insomnia is a house with too much to say.

~

I take care of a man whose brain gets him out of bed every two hours or so. He thinks it is morning. "Look at your clock B—" I tell him. "It is only 2:14 AM, it's only midnight, it's only ..." Sometimes he thinks he has to get ready for school. He thinks he's in high school, he thinks he's getting ready to work, the work he did years ago in Alaska working on the fishing boats. He's 24, he's 15. "No B—, you are 46." "Really? Where does it all go?"

~

I read somewhere that we spend one third of our life sleeping. No wonder my daughter does not want to fall asleep. I've worked third shift for so many years. I sleep when the doves are cooing in the rafters. I sleep after the children board the bus. I sometimes can't sleep for days, because of work and responsibilities. Some of you can't understand this, some of you know exactly what I mean. To be so tired, makes me think of tires on a truck, forever rolling forward down an endless highway, spewing exhaust, exhausted, what is spent, and when one is too tired eventually from this life, exhaust is what can be inhaled, hook up the tube and shut the garage door and then you are, as they say, up there with the angels.

~

Insomnia literally means to be in a negative state of *somus*, the Latin for sleep, which is related to the Greek *hypnos*, who traveled between realms. Night passes sleepless into day, and one must get ready for work, as if hypnotized, nodding one's head like an addict. Why does heroin have a hero inside it? What is its superpower? Perhaps the erasure of the world like winter, handing out the long O of loss? The world slowly slips away as the clenched fist unfurls.

~

To be walking down a street calling for home, as in the dreams my youngest daughter often has, the ones that wake her crying for her mother. My oldest daughter says, *I can't sleep, give me a pill.* She never has nightmares. I think of slipping her a Trazodone, or the whiskey mothers would add to milk in the old country, where to count sheep was to save them from the dream of wolves.

~

Give me a pill we say for every malady. The snowdrift of our falling lids. The insomnia of winter, erasing the world. To be this tired should be illegal, my co-worker said as he was finishing a double shift. Insomnia of the desk clerk. Insomnia at the two-star hotel. Insomnia of the fisherman, or is it the fish, in the barbed moonlight?

~

I used to sing old Irish songs to my daughters to lull them to sleep when they were younger. Now, they would rather watch videos of strange dubbed Russian women making homemade makeup on YouTube, or the mad scientist who teaches kids ways to make moth balls flame. I find my daughters asleep eventually, dreaming with the flickering blue light on their faces, like old people in the nursing homes nodding in front of *I Love Lucy*, guiding them into dreams, all the detritus and dead celebrities of another century when they were raised. Towards morning, the garbage trucks arrive, lifting their loads in the still black AM. The ambulance drives by with its silent siren.

~

The older we get the less we sleep, as if we know we have so little to hold on to, or maybe just because we have to piss. Insomnia shares the same root with the Spanish *sueno*, which means to dream. The insomnia of a closed cinema. *Sueno*, which reminds me of *cielo*, which is sky, we could dream ourselves into the house of the sky, but the floorboards have too much to say.

~

Sky we take from the Norse and sleep is from the German *sleps, slap,* or the German *dose,* or the Old English *drowsy,* which is perhaps closest to how it feels to walk to sleep. Which is why I suppose most overdoses the paramedics tell me happen in the AM.

~

The sound of my daughter sleeping is a soft wind through the tall reeds. A sound that could save me. I never feel I "fall" to sleep, but walk to sleep, as if down to the underworld to visit my dead, or through a door in the room I walk through, and there I am in a city both familiar and strange that exists only when I close my eyes, with its alleyways and endless parapets, and the rooms, closer to the rooms of my childhood, that I always return to. But tonight, nothing can help. Not even the rain

~

longing for the dark. I have walked into a painting by Edward Hopper: a man awake in a chair in a blue room. All the nighthawks bend over coffee at the diner. The waitress is brewing another pot. The ER nurses out on break, the blue smoke of menthols rises in the parking lot light. This is the time all our dead return.

~

"What worries do you have to keep you up?" I say to my daughter. I do not ask her about her mother, who I now admit is at the hospital again. She says, "Anyways, I took a nap today." She's wide awake. I say, "Eat something, drink some milk." The insomnia of a glass of milk. The insomnia of the waiting room. A house full of votive candles. A house full of whispers.

~

What parent does not live in a house full of whispers after the children have gone to bed? Everyone is now asleep but the father, who hears only a mosquito buzzing. He stares at the pile of bills on the desk. He walks quietly down the stairs. He cannot find the children. He cannot find his wife. He was to leave for work an hour ago. The phone is out of order. Outside fire trucks have arrived. The neighbor's house is burning down. A sound like a cat drowning. He is walking away from his life down an empty road so long and straight he can see the curve of the earth.

~

What do I have to hock at the pawnbroker of sleep? The boat is docked at the quay. How many nights my only company is the rain? Do the trees ever sleep? Do they dream of the long winter, or the fullness of their leaves? I hear them tapping on the roof. My wife said for years she never remembered her dreams, and then after a certain age she did. When we dream, are we really living two lives? I used to have a Russian blue cat who would climb into bed with me and twitch. She left before dawn. I imagined she was dreaming of robins. What songs she ate as she slept. When I awoke the bed was full of feathers, I thought an angel had come to visit me, until I saw the dead bird my cat had brought me in the bed like a gift. Insomnia is the murderer of sleeping doves.

~

All my children coo when they dream. My wife sometimes talks in her sleep. I can trick her into conversations. I ask her, what does the rain say? She says, "I have traveled across many mountains." Far off in the distance I hear the sirens. She says, "Honey the tea kettle is whistling."

~

The father says, "I cannot sleep because every time I close my eyes, I hear an elegy." The old ones have gathered in the eaves. Horses and elephants sleep standing. For years I drank vodka because I could not find sleep. Too often I heard the floorboards of my childhood. Those were decades I never dreamed. Elusiveness was a word the future earned. I thought for sure by now I would be dead before I would be the age I am. Perhaps it is my wife who saved me? Despite the odds and evidence? Sometimes in the middle of the night my wife will wake and go and smoke in the garage. She walks heavy on her four-toed foot. She shapes the shadows.

What is she thinking then, quiet in the long O of alone. Sometimes I watch her from the door, adrift in her long uncombed hair, the smoke rising from her mouth like noir. She says, "I would prefer to be the letter b. Not for the buzz, but for the blur. Or the d of doze." I tell her, "I would like to be the silent e that makes a vowel long, like the way the Irish purse their mouths and pronounce love."

5

Frida Kahlo

I want to write a sonnet about Frida Kahlo's orange trees, the ones that fed her before her accident and after, the same tree weighed with fruit that reached for her, but my own wife is in the hospital today because she has been choreographing herself towards a slow suicide after she survived a decade of illness. She was admitted for pain to the hospital this week— I found 19 little bottles, you know the kind you might get on an airplane if you were flying to visit the garden of Frida Kahlo,

bottles of cinnamon whiskey she hides in our daughter's toy bucket of stuffed unicorns, bears, a monkey, a panda, and three large bottles of red wine, two drank to the dregs. I do not judge my wife. My wife is in a lot of pain. I called her, and they have her on an IV, and when I see her in her hospital bed, the way I have visited for many years, I can't help but think of Frida Kahlo lying in her bed of blood and herbs after her accident, her spine damaged, her painting where she rests with a monkey and a cat on her shoulder, not stuffed ones

like in my daughter's bucket. My daughter who talks on the phone to her mother and asks with that tremulous voice when she will come home. Perhaps it is that sound that will save my wife? The sound of missing, a sound so tiny. Like the sound of the tiny umbrella that Frida Kahlo lost to the wind and went to find and was hit by a bus, the silent absence after the death of Frida Kahlo who no longer moved through the garden, dead by an embolism but the gardeners, the workers with names I cannot find, went on and watered the cactus pear, trimmed the thorny bougainvillea and the orange tree, their brown callused hands tended to her spirit that entered the earth of Casa Azul as one afternoon Frida Kahlo sat up, after decades of pain, she pushed herself paint-spattered out of bed, and she walked to the window and opened the curtains. My wife will walk out of that hospital today. With her prescriptions for pain meds and the green and blue bruises on her arms from the IV. Once after her accident,

Frida Kahlo wrote an imaginary birth certificate for the child she miscarried. She named him Leonardo. She baptized him after a year. The losses my wife carries are not imaginary. *Sangrente corazon.* I try to stop the bleeding with the bandages of my hands. Our daughter's sister sucked from her body, the years of wounds and hospitals. She wears a shawl of dark light around her shoulders, like the shawl of Frida Kahlo.

She sits alone in the empty rooms of our house, and she drinks until the pain recedes, until the pain returns. Today, she limped out of the hospital doors, a nurse holding her arm, like a young Frida Kahlo, and I swear I saw all around her in her hair were black butterflies.

Death Letter #4: first he takes the smallest things

The katydid. The lady bug's lament. Husked carapace we find. The ants the children crush and finger. It is there death wants and lingers. The small tortures that we tender. The petals wilt long before the winter. The deer frozen in the ice. The car that skids and sinks beneath the lake. The hollow hole of breath on glass. And still I dream of all those losses along the way to old, OD or accident. There is a place I hear full of tiny wings beneath the veil, the way the trees hide cicada sirens or the weeds the cricket's high call. See the Plains' grass part as if without a wind. These are the deaths we thought we did not notice, but we've carried them all along, the second we step out of the carapace of our bodies we start to sing and rise. Our husked skin cracks open spilling music as if we were filled with cellos. Or milkweed, spilling seeds of light—

After Tolstoy

The man has a mark under his left eye, a small abrasion, cut as if from his fingernail. Did you scratch yourself in your sleep? "No," he says, and touches the mark with two fingers. "It was the bird," he says. "I was dreaming the bird came. But the bird wouldn't sing. The bird said, 'I will leave you a birthmark. This is how we will know you when you are born again with wings.'"

The man brings me a bowl

and asks what he should put in it today. We do this every Saturday morning. He told his case worker he wants to collect things to help with his memory, so she recommended stamps or coins, but somewhere along the chain of command probably from the occupational therapist who is kind of brilliant, it was changed to have him collect something weekly. So now every Saturday the man brings me his bowl, a big blue plastic bowl, and we decide what today he will collect. Last Saturday it was raining so he grabbed his umbrella and went outside and when he returned he proudly announced he had collected a bowl of rain. Then he raised it to his lips and drank. Another rainy Saturday he returned with a bowl of earth worms he had carefully collected from the sidewalk. No, he did not eat them, but we saved them, and he went fishing with his stoned brother who came to visit the next day and they returned with a bucket of fish they wanted me to clean, but um, I said we can't do that, state regulations. I lied. I had no idea how to clean those fish and wasn't even sure they were edible, they looked like deformed carp, one had three eyes. In June the man returned with a bowl of dandelion heads. It looked like a bowl of miniature murdered sunflowers. In May I saw him stamping the ground and he brought in a bowl of dead ants. No, we didn't eat them. One day to my horror he returned with a bowl of tiny shards of broken glass he found in the greenhouse we abandoned after a big oak fell on it years ago. But most days he finds sticks, a few stones, maybe some candy wrappers that someone dropped, a plastic ring, a rusty spring to an unnamed thing, a handful of bent nails, once a brown shoe maybe a resident had taken off and left on the grass, too many cigarette butts. He said "I hate litterers." Most of his finds were the simple detritus that a child might pick up and put in a box of treasures, only this is a forty-six year old man, out getting his exercise, a little sun working his memory. Many days he finds nothing. One Sunday he simply sat outside, returned empty-handed, and said, "I brought you a bowl of prayers." In autumn, when the world was dying, he brought the expected: rubied leaves, acorns, "a bowl of helicopters," maple seeds, unhusked buckeyes we opened and then shined and roasted. Laurel branches he said, "We can weave into a crown because I'm kind of like Jesus. I came back from the dead." In late summer he went out, said it was too hot and sat down by the raised flower beds along the edge of our building. A half hour later I saw him outside talking to himself. When he turned, it looked like he was breaking off sprigs of forsythia, husks of milkweed, maybe to make "a bowl of flowers" and later I saw some slight motion of light or wind in his hands. What the hell is that? I walked outside. What do you have there? "See," he said, "a bowl of lepidoptera." I saw contently fluttering among the sprigs of golden forsythia were the black and orange wings of two monarchs and a tiger-striped swallowtail. How in the world did he get them to stay! "M, you are the butterfly whisperer for sure." In winter, he brought bowl after bowl of snow to the porch. "What are you collecting there?" I asked. "Snowman heads." One winter night after dinner when it was wicked cold out, I saw him emerge from his room with his coat on. I just thought he was going out to smoke. I watched him standing still. Then I saw he was holding his bowl above his head. He looked sculptural, this gentle fat six-foot Italian man, who had survived being hit by a truck, years of rehab, who had to relearn how to tie his shoes. If ever I was moved it was in that moment. Soon he would be able to leave and return to life with his older sister and her husband. Every day he was getting better, naming more things, remembering what week, month, year it was. His sense of time was good. He would still need help. He couldn't do a shopping list on his own and numbers for some reason never added up anymore, and sometimes he thought he was twenty years younger. He'd need help with his insulin. But he could fix himself a sandwich. He liked to watch the news. He forgot names, but who doesn't. Soon he would walk away back towards something part the past and part a future we all could hope for but no one except him could have scripted. If I could give him a bowl to take with him back to the world, what would I put in it? A bowl of patience. A bowl of mercy. Directions to forget his life before, or to remember, or even to find comfort in the absences he has gained. Absences he can fill each day with a bowl of new unimagined gifts. When he returned from the yard that evening, he was staring down between his hands. His eyes were strange and distant. I asked what do you have there, M? I don't see anything in your bowl. It's empty. "No it's not," he said. "What are you blind? Can't you see it? Can't you see my bowl of starlight?"

The Familiar Things of this World

The rebirth of this earth will be orchestrated in minor chords, so we remember what was lost and given. I read these words penned in the margin of a book I was reading, and damned if I know where they came from, some anonymous notation in this book about war in land my ancestors farmed decades before they were written. So I recall the shtetl and the Rebbe and the black earth and my great uncle who made violins. In the book I am reading, there is a man, the son of a Rebbe, a partisan who refuses to give up a violin, he plays when they are far from the farms for his men, he says this is the sound of what is being erased, wears it slung in a case on his back with his submachine gun. It might as well be a bow, or a sword, or a spear. For so much of us are these false appendages of furious fists. But yesterday I saw a man in the woods talking to a tree. I startled him when I turned onto the path so much I too grew a little nervous. He stared at me. I stood. I said, "I talk to the trees too, sometimes they say a word or two." He was a tall man, black and gray hair and beard, dressed in an old green army jacket, good boots on his feet. He said, "I didn't hear you coming. Guess I'm not what I used to be." He said, "I was distracted, looking up at the trees." He said, "My name is Harry." He said, "I hike out here to listen." He said he had been to the war. He said he had been to the war and returned for three tours in the next one. "What fool does that?" he said. "I guess I thought I was invincible, but I didn't know the wounds inside I'd hidden never fully heal." He said he didn't think he could make it here, and then he said, "My counselor, this good woman, she told me of a man who took up the violin after the great war. She said the man couldn't play a note for a long time, but he hid outside by the stream for an hour a day and he played, and as he played the war went away for a while. He played, she said, outside in the woods by this stream. I wanted to meet that man who went to war and came back to play music. But she said you can't meet him; he is dead, she said. He wasn't much for words anyways, she said. She almost couldn't get the words out, she said it was her father. I didn't know what to say to her then. I said the usual things we say when someone tells us someone they loved has died—I'd be a terrible counselor, I wasn't much to my kids either. I didn't say anything to help because what was there to say. But that evening I came out here and I swear ever since, when I close my eyes, I hear that old soldier strumming some meager tune on his cheap fiddle, each note bringing him back to his daughter and to the familiar things of this world. The trees hear it too. It's like he's inside them, or maybe it is the violin inside them that we can hear. Close your eyes son, close your eyes and you might hear him." And we both did, and as we both stood there, the wind blew a minor third right through the door in my chest.

The Bringer of Things

What is the wind? What does it bring? Some nights it brings me hunger. Some nights it sings like a voice from a cabaret in a faraway *arrondissement*. Some nights it brings me hand-knitted mittens, the cold, and creases. Some nights the bones of my dead, the old building rattles like the bones of my dead. The wind might bring me a switchblade, or a souffle. Tourniquets of cut gloves, the scent of forsythia in late summer, the drowsy blouse of bees. My fortune told in fish entrails and coffee grinds. It brings me amulets and alms, and what I've been owed which is nothing less than what I've earned.

After the wind brings a dream the wind dies down, brings the man to a wake. He asks, "Is that the train coming to take me away?" I tell him the time for his departure is a long time coming. I tell him it is only the wind riding the rails. The wind asks me to say the name of my great-grandmother who died coughing one winter night when the wind was a wolf. The wind asks me for the name of my great-grandfather who let her die, who married her cousin, who sat Shiva for his own son. Tell us the wind says, bear witness, and we will bring you salves for your sorrows. Write her name in the black earth. Tell us the wind demands, and we will bring you whiskey and clover. You will erase her name, I tell the wind. Bring me a ration of salt, bring me cut garlic and drawers of cloves. What does the wind ask of us anyways, but to stand against it? We will blow you aside said the wind, we erase mountains. We level forests. In the distance I hear the train riding through the thick snow, carrying its freight of factory-made things, its carloads of migrants. Who of them is sleeping? The man is awake now. "Is that our train? Do you have our tickets?" He is just a man, "As just a man as Noah."

"The train will be here soon," I tell the man. "Get dressed, put on your best clothes. And good walking shoes. The train will only take us as far as the last station."

The Hardest Part

"What are you thinking about?" he said. She was sitting at the table, playing with her feeding tube. Staring out at the robins on the lawn. It was early spring after a hard rain. The crocuses were in bloom. She had just gotten the children off to school. They sat with coffee. But she was far away, the way she often was. "I was thinking," she said, "of things we have to learn backwards." "Like what?" he said. He wasn't good at these sorts of questions. He thought he was always being tested even if he wasn't. She on the other hand was terrific at all kinds of verbal games. She could make up riddles on the spot, pun any word sending their daughters into bent-over hysterics. "Well," she said, "our laces. We have to learn to untie our shoes before can learn to tie them." He said, "Oh," and thought back to when he was small. How his mother would put her hand over his to guide his hand into the loops. And even then what was most fun was pulling the string. He hated shoes. He wanted to walk barefoot everywhere. "So," she said, "love is this way." He got out of his own head and looked at her: radiant with a thin fierce light illness had honed. "Well, love is this way," she said. "Before you really learn to love someone." She said, "It is easy to fall in love, so easy. A glance, a question. But loving someone? And learning not to? How do you learn to not love someone? How do you let someone go? It's backwards, see? We have to learn heartbreak before we can ever learn to love." He looked at her, half joked, "is that why you were so awful to me for years." "Yes," she said. "You're so stupid. I was teaching you how to love." He realized in that moment something left his chest, some dark breath of resentment he had convinced himself was grief. How many years had they sat there? Outside the robin flew up into the oak where it was building its nest. A crow played with a dead thing out in the street. This was the labor of life. She was right. To live, things died, branches break, twigs blown by the winter wind. So much of being alive was like this, backwards in reserve, winter into autumn, summer into spring, he saw it all, saw her after the last surgery, tied to tubes and machines, saw her before she was sick, saw her drunk undressing in a slow dance, saw her in the hospital rooms, their children's tiny heads, saw her leaving to work in her uniform, counting her tips after a double shift at the table, saw her before he knew her, climbing onto a factory roof because she could, a nine-year-old climbing, until the police arrived to talk her down. Heard her first cries. Saw her parents driving to work in the factories before she was born. Saw her in the moon over the old country, head-scarved women beating hides, singing the old songs side by side, in the old tongue, bending into the river to let go the black cloaks, baskets on their strong hips, the children gathering sticks under the thatched roof where one daughter died, where the babushkas knitted, where the fire burned in the black stove. He saw her from the hayfields at dusk, waving to him to come home for *kolajca*, for dinner, then she was gone, into the door, as the dark wrapped its arms around his shoulders.

After Ibn Arabi

The man tells me not to turn on the television. He says, "I want to sit alone in the dark," even though the communal area has a couple lamps on, is dim; it does have a good feeling to it with the overhead fluorescents off after 11 PM, it feels more like a home and not an institution, ironically when nearly everyone is in their rooms and beds. Now it is 5 AM and the man is up early, an hour before we serve breakfast. Outside it is 58 degrees in February, when the average temperature should be 28 degrees. Lately, nothing is as it should be. The man says he doesn't want the noise from the television. He says he just wants to sit. "I want to sit and drink my water." The man is schizophrenic. He tells me often about the noise in his head, so when he says he wants to sit without sound, I get it. He can be frightening. He can be sweet as they say, as a peach. This morning he has his own eyes. On bad nights he gets the eyes of a man neither of us know. I walk through a door to the office to finish my paperwork. I peek back in a few minutes to see how the man is doing. He is sitting straight—back on the couch, eyes open staring ahead. He doesn't look anxious or waiting for anything. No psalm or sorrowing, but only to sit as if to sit is nothing more and nothing less. The man is *alone with the alone.* No one is telling him what to do. He cups his cup of water in his hands. The water trembles slightly from his palsy as if by wind. The only sound the present tense of human breath.

As if Translated from the Ukrainian

"I pick up my footprints."
Vasyl Holoborodko

I pick up the mud around the print and put it in my pocket.
I pick up the hand shape in the snow of my daughter's hand.
She is now grown. I pick up a toy I lost when I was seven. I
found it under the bed of my dead aunt. I pick up the bed and
lay in it to hear her last dreams, the few words that dripped
like morphine from her mouth at the end. I pick up my dead
aunt. My dead father. My dead mother. I wrap the leash of
every dead dog we had: Egor the Siberian Huskey. Alina his
sister, pulling the red sled my son rode to a job far from here.
I pick up the miles he is away, one by one, and put them into
a satchel, with the leashes I've wrapped into a noose. I put
the chandelier in there in case I need somewhere to hang
myself. I put my neck in there. I pick up _____ empty,
a sort of sound, or lack of sound ____ I pick ____ a ____
dandelion, when I was a child, we called them wish flowers.
Or was that my daughter, blowing on them _____ the lawn
covered with a thousand tiny suns.

Fugue of Sudden Mercies that We Make

"Who can predict the world's sudden mercies?"
Joseph Millar

The woman is pissed because she can't have a bowl of cereal until the nurse comes to check her blood sugar. "The fucking nurse," the woman says, "never comes at the same time. I always have to fucking wait." The nurse is a bastard, I sympathize in my head. I say why don't you go smoke and I'll fill up your travel cup with coffee. This brightens her but when I return to the table two minutes later with her coffee, she is angry—"Aren't you going to get my cereal maybe after I smoke you can have it ready when I come back in." She's completely forgotten the conversation we just had. She forgets so many things—even her three children she left twenty years ago for her pills and the bottle, forgets falling face first into a glass coffee table, forgets the overdoses and coma, years become months, months become a day. What is a day of sudden mercies? What is to remember when remembrance is loss? This unnamable place, small as a bowl of cereal, endlessly empty. What bowl without pity she spoons into her mouth. I watch her walk slow, her knee hurt when drunk she walked out into traffic, she walks slow out into the sudden mercy of the small rain to smoke. The nurse will be late again, and her anger will grow. She is a stout woman on the other side of fifty. "I didn't want to live," she said. And walked into an oncoming car. She told us this when she arrived, but it wasn't in her paperwork. Her last overdose wasn't an accident either. She sips her coffee black, listening to the morning news and weather. I take out a deck of cards and she brightens again. "Tomorrow," I tell her," I can start checking your sugar, so this is the last day you will have to wait." "The last place I was at said the same thing. Tomorrow

tomorrow everything was tomorrow." Is impatience for the next day a good thing? I think so, I want to tell her you are looking ahead. You want it now. You want to be a person who breathes, a person who leaves this place to sit when you want. She used to have her own apartment. She drank a fifth of vodka a day. Today I slip her a bowl of sweetened cereal before the nurse arrives. The nurse eyes me suspiciously looking at the woman's elevated blood sugar. What is a bowl of cereal when it can become a bowl of erasure, a bowl of sudden mercies? The woman lifted the bowl and drank the sugary milk when the cereal was gone, the milk turned slightly blue. A bowl of sky she drank. I would give this woman the moon to swallow like a eucharist if I could, but she is long past the problematics of faith. Her father, himself in his late seventies, is her guardian. He visits and brings her cigarettes, listens to her long litanies of I wants, I want to go homes. But where is home for her? Where has it been for a decade? A quart of vodka? The erasure of pills? Men who she didn't know she brought home who robbed and beat her? Who will bear witness for what we call unto ourselves is not a home but a far and brutal travel? The cathedral of sorrows we cannot even bend our broken knees to pray in. I want to go home she says, and her mind flips through the rolodex of decades, she crosses against the light and into traffic. She is more than the filigree of scars that lace her. She beats everyone at cards and backgammon, late into the evening. Forgive whatever leaves us still must speak. Sometimes for reasons she cannot tell she sleeps with her lights on. Perhaps, it is as Antonio Porchia wrote, "Sometimes at night I light a lamp so as not to see." What is the dark but a place to lay your head, a place to name the dead. But she lays her head on a pillow of light, a pillow of erasure. In the distance, the endless freight trains haul their loads of goods along the rails that rim the lake, on toward Cleveland and Chicago, the ache and heave of them fills the morning air. The woman asks me for a bowl of cereal. It is another day. I hand her a cup of black coffee. This time I offer my arm and we walk slowly out the door. There is freezing rain, falling like elegies across the grounds. I watch her as she holds the rail with one hand and walks down the steps, steps slowly to the bench under the awning and sits down. "Look," she says pointing behind us. And there we witness the delicate frozen filigree of the rain freezing against the windows. How it shines. What we've failed, does it matter? If we can't remember? The hurt we've caused. The absences we've spent. To forget what is owed and will not be forgiven. Is this a kind of mercy? I hear the groan and ache of tree limbs bearing a brutal weight. The woman looks up suddenly as if to speak. All around us, the world has turned to glass.

The Frog Singers Group

I'm not sure how it started. It predates my arrival at the facility though legend has it began when a traveling therapist from the state or corporate recommended we start a singing program to stimulate our residents' damaged neurons and our director said, "Sure that sounds great! Who's going to pay for their lessons? Who's going to teach them, the birds?"

Now at night we gather the selected residents. If it is warm they like to come out in their nightgowns, you know the old-fashioned kind, the women in ankle-length Amish-sewn dresses with white lace eyelet trim, the men in their slim cotton sleeping caps and button-up shirts, their full-bodied thermals with the trap door in the back. All except for R, who likes to wear his full Adidas running suit for twenty-four hours. We gather out on the lawn and wait for the last of dusk to descend, there is an anticipation as we look out to the line of trees and the marsh that borders the facility and the winding creek just beyond the edge. First we hear a few full-throated croaks, deep in the larynx, which our residents in near unison answer, then a few fast high trills. Our people are old, as oaks or weeping willows. So they sit in lawn chairs as if waiting for the rain. P stands and lets go a deep omom pah in response to a bullfrog mating call. Our people now begin to bellow in discordant union. These are love songs. It has been this way since the first fire. Our people sing till they can no more. We check their O2 levels with pulsometers. We guide them slowly back to bed. They walk with the silence of the snails. How the joy flows through their blood. They sleep that night like newborns. A small rain falls. The walkways writhe with worms. The dark folds its arms around my shoulders. Nothing born on this strange planet is a stranger.

Photocopying Memories

On third shift I've been given the job to photocopy memories. The memories are gathered through spoken report by the first shift staff. This is part of a participant's rehab. We have them write or recite a memory each week and staff transcribes it. The ones with worse frontal lobe damage tell the same memory. This is called looping. But with a little prodding, a little questioning, and sometimes using photos—who is this? Do you remember how old you were? Was it winter? Is your mother singing? Can you sing that song? Did your father smoke cigars a lot? Did you?—the staff can get them someplace new, a new detail, which is of course not new but old and hidden way down inside them. At night then I make copies of the handwritten notes and place the photocopy in the participant's weekly file. I try to place it into a participant's file immediately so as not to mix them up. But once I did just that. Then again. How photocopying and reading them they'd begun to seep into my brain as if they were mine. I'd tell a story and then say, wait that isn't me. This gave me an idea. How often have you done that? One day there was the avocational therapist reading D's memory to J who began to remember this life she didn't have until she did. I remember, she said. I remember. What is more powerful than that? And what harm can a few false memories do for those who have lost many? I know the day staff will catch on soon. But we've had so much turn-over lately. It has now been weeks. Please don't tell. You have to understand, you who have a past. You whose memories you claim as yours—how much of your story is another's life? And anyways, what are words but things that cannot be fixed. Even what is fabricated becomes much more than marginalia if we believe it as our own. If you could witness B start to tell a memory over breakfast and K will jump in, that's just like me! And in this way, they who were unheard now hear enraptured and clap and weep for each is the protagonist of the same stories.

My favorite words are small like dirt

Rain that turns to sleet across the muddy trench along the rural highway. Words like plow or hay, sun, or shape. My favorite words are small like dirt. My dead come around this way. They wear the clean pressed shirts we buried them in, their favorite Sunday dress. My favorite words are small like dirt, like dig. Words like steel and echo, like holler and hole. A dark we peer down, calling. Anyone down there, we say? Waiting for another voice to sing. Words like mine, and lamp light, head lamp and edge water, lake or grit, stream or sinker. Song, or shard. Words like weed, the ones my daughter picks, wilted stems with blossoms, and gives them to her mother. Words like wife, and hold. Words like nap, and lung. Not words like impossible. Not words like chemotherapy. My favorite words are small, they taste like dirt. Have you ever eaten dirt? The sweetness of red dirt. Breast milk or broth. Milk bottle. Milk glass. Not cataract. Not insulin. Not neurodegenerative. Not pernicious. Not amenia. Well amenia is a beautiful word. It sounds like a flower. A blood red flower. That turns pale, like a lily on a windowsill in winter light. Snow falling, and the old couple out walking, arm in arm, up a hill. When I turn away they've become clouds. Sky. There is a window in the sky. When we die, we walk right through it. My daughter tells me it is a small window. Did I tell you clouds is her favorite word.

5 AM After Reading Roethke

My daughter often wakes and cannot sleep, she talks to me in the bedroom doorway, chattering about her nose is stuffed or she had to pee and now it is still dark though day approaches, she hovers in the doorway saying she thought I was at work, didn't know it was my night off, what day is it, and I hesitate to remind her of the afternoon's obligations, her school meetings and work. Let the morning unfold, the blessed dark recede around her easy before she must give her hours to strangers who do not love her. She is wrapped in a blanket. She is nearly tall as her mother, who is too often like this week at the hospital, wrapped in her own quilt of pain and absence from our arms. But her mother will return as we all return to anyplace that is as far from harm as we can help which isn't much these days. Our daughter closes the door but always after I say the words we all say in our language that mean we are each other's despite anything. She says a few more sentences quietly that I can't hear through the door, chattering away as much to herself as to her father who has trouble hearing her high-pitched sing-song phonemes that travel through the hall. I often wonder if it is a kind of riddle only she can answer, one I hope we never fully solve, a chattering sort of something part, perhaps, the wake of the other world we carry upon waking, the way I wish I could translate what the mourning doves inscribe upon the dew and dawn now offering their notations across the trees and wires, as our daughter sits to read, quietly chirping a perfectly familiar noise, like the birds, that is not quite singing, more light yellow and magenta, mixed with cerulean and texture, grass and tulip leaves, letters of twigs and pieces of trash and twine weaved into nests, the not-yet-born they warm beneath their wings a kind of writing on the wind is what language can never fully reach. As our daughter will remain unknowable she says a sentence or two, punctuated with the sound of her own feet walking away. A few syllables merely noise. Fragile as a blue egg. A sound so small I hold it in my fist.

One Sentence on Pain

I wanted to write one sentence about pain I woke up and my knee and back ached from the cool fan and I was trying to explain it to my wife who said her stomach hurt and my father in law limped in with one elbow bent into an el on his back and pushed us all out of the way with his slow I can't see anyone else in the world walk and his hearing aids left on the bedroom counter to make his morning toast and jelly and our daughter was doing her morning pacing back and forth that made me ask her do your ankles ever hurt as I worry about feet since her brother was born with an ankle deformity that makes his feet stick out like some marvelous aquatic creature and her sister was born with hip dysphasia and shortened muscles so she walks up on her toes like a constant ballerina about to go into pointe but no no she says my daughter her feet never hurt though she says my eyes hurt and I say why do your eyes hurt and she says because I'm looking at your face and I raise my hand and joke I'll teach you about respect for the elderly I'll teach you about pain which was of course the initial thesis but she's already running away laughing she is so fast she could probably win the special Olympics or the regular one she has so little feeling for pain at least the physical kind which I read is common with Asperger's children, though I know she feels a pain a long aloneness at times when she was growing up but now she has a lot of friends the girls her age in the neighborhood who oddly seem to cling to each other's eccentricities a sort of tribal protectiveness against the things of this world so I know at least these years, these brutal years with her mother often in the hospital where they ask her mother about her pain what number is your pain and is there a number she once shouted that means just shoot me and I said like horses which made her laugh and the nurse laughed a little and

then they gave her some morphine which if you go off it too
soon will cause you immense pain as the pain of the world
which has no number for even though it is in the body pain
is an abstraction like the cold my wife asks me is the room
cold and I say no I'm not cold and she says I think it's freez-
ing it's not not freezing when I say I'm ok it's an abstraction
temperature to a point of perception that can be measured
measured to dismiss what you feel to quantify your suffering
and give it a shape so when she says she's cold and I put the
blanket on her and I put my arms around her shoulders and
press my body against hers giving her my degrees and how
every day I can only hope in the same way I can take some
of the pain she carries and add it to my own the pain of this
world which is why I tell my daughter we are here not for
ourselves and she said I'm not here for you I'm here for the
snacks I know she is one of the shards of light from the first
vessel shattered that we are and that these words, well I don't
know if I ever got to what I wanted to say, except to say we
laugh together despite the pain and if I ever knew or know
except to tell you a stranger out there suffering you are not
alone and despite the aches and growing old let us wheel or
cane or limp out of the rain and the ground covered with
worms and the dark earth drowning let us sit simply on the
unfolded chairs under the awning and tell stories of the peo-
ple we were and if we moan or cough it will be shared and
never any of us the kind of people who shoot horses.

The Window

I want to make a poem like a brick she said, uh huh, he said, only half listening. He was watching the game. It was a really big game he would tell someone long after. Uh huh. Then she bent her head and started writing. She wrote like the ancient ones, putting a sharpened pencil to a piece of paper pressed from a tree. She wrote and wrote, and then out of the corner of his eye he saw her folding the paper. Hey, she said, uh huh, he said, waiting for the next down. Hey, she said, a little louder, who are you? Really? Hey look at me, look at me for Christ's sake, and then he turned, that was when she threw it, threw that poem like a brick and it shattered the shut window he had in his chest. Pieces of him flickered and refracted the blue light of the television on the living room floor. Air and light filtered into his body. Psalms of finches he had never paid attention to. A small green iridescent insect. The smell of TV dinners. There he was at five years old, being beaten. There he was at seventeen on that Greyhound bus. He stood with this gaping hole in his chest. He couldn't speak. The game wasn't even close and the announcers on the TV were asking trivia questions. She walked forward, stretched the hole out with her arms and—what did she do next? Well, she climbed in. She climbed right inside his body. The room became a room of absence. Who am I now, he said? Who were you then, she said, or should I say he told us this story, a long time later out mowing his lawn, a little voice said to him, says to him every day, every time he looks at her, and he pointed back to the house where she waved, or was it when he pointed at his chest where she stood in the window, sunlight streaming from somewhere deep inside him.

Eulogy at my Own Wake after The Golden Girls

At the residential facility I work at we watch *The Golden Girls* every Saturday morning at 6:30 AM, right after breakfast. We watch it as a compromise with L who used to snatch the clicker out of anyone's hand and change the channel. He thinks the Common Area is his, which it is we tell him, but it is everyone else's too. Rather than fighting with him all the time I suggested, why don't we keep the clicker with staff and make a TV "schedule." Everyone was like, that's a great idea! Why didn't we think of that? Because sometimes the solution is right there and it's hard to see. Sometimes the problem is not the person but the things around us, the thing which we are fighting over. I learned this in every relationship I have been in. Often it is not the person, it's the object and act that needs to be resolved. Of course, you cannot just give your screaming children away, so sometimes you need to find a different answer. As a parent I learned they are fighting over a toy, remove the toy and send them outside to play. I do not know if this is the way to be, but what can we ever really know about anything. It is all trial and guess and we just hope in the end for a little bit of praise. On *The Golden Girls* this morning Estelle Getty who plays Sophia, the mother, decides to have her own wake. She says she went to her friend Sal's wake and they "Said such beautiful things about him, but he was not there to hear them. Because he was dead!" She said, "I want to be able to hear what people say about me while I'm still alive." She convinces the other women to organize a wake for her and invite all her friends. The people show up, no one is eating Betty White's pastries, instead they are crying all over the strudel, and then Sophia appears, and says, "Do you like my dress?" The shocked faces, and one woman says, "I took off work and drove 30 miles to get here and you didn't even have the decency to die?"

There are no extravagant eulogies, no speeches of what Sophia meant. After everyone is gone, Sophia says, "You three couldn't even get my wake right, now I'll never get to hear the things they'd say." And her sitcom daughter Bea Arthur says, "Well, think of this: everyone we invited showed up." Isn't that enough to know the ones you loved will arrive to bless you farewell? And if I was at my own wake, I'd offer up my own soliloquy of all the things I've failed. Failed to be patient with the rain, failed to tend the garden in late summer, failed to listen to my daughter when she was trying to tell me of some teenage pain. Failed to say it is ok. Failed to learn the names of those tiny white butterflies, or different kinds of bees, or the names for my father's lures. Failed to make time if time can be made. Failed to put the dishes away. Failed to forget the grievances or remember the anniversaries of the small hours. Failed to make them linger. Failed to blow on my soup. Failed to share my burns. Failed to re-piece the shards. Failed to count the fireflies. Failed to notice the day the forsythia bloomed. Failed to listen. Failed to sing. Failed to say how the people in my life shimmered. Like the lake in late summer. I failed to drown. And for no reason I can name I think of my son when he was three and after it rained he'd go for walks with me and his mother, stomping in every puddle we passed, he in his big yellow oversized boots.

Whatever Happened to David Caruso

What if what you are running from is the moment when you found out your life was much worse than you suspected? It was the first night my wife hadn't had a drink in weeks; we were up watching episodes of CSI Miami, as she tossed and turned. CSI that great cheesy 2000s cop show, when she says, "What ever happened to David Caruso?" 90s redhead tough guy cop whose acting career hit a snag in a series of B movies until he found his role as detective Horatio Caine in CSI Miami. He always had a tagline, to open and close a scene: a body could be lying there, and the coroner looks up at the sky and says, "No one falls three stories and gets up and runs away," and Horatio Caine puts on those mirrored sunglasses and says, "If you do, you have something to hide."

Which makes me think of one of Caruso's early roles, as a loud young cop out to nail Christopher Walken's ultimate gangster Frank White in the classic gangster flick *Kings of New York*. When at a police funeral, White rolls up in a limo, says, "Hey you," and in front of a hundred cops, blasts a shotgun into Caruso's face.

Which is what it feels like the moment when you find out your life was much worse than you suspected.

It is like that isn't it with the poets with their academic predicures and their summer rendezvous at Bread Loaf and their endowed professorships and endless complaints about who got what job. I can't help but hear Biggie, who called himself the Black Frank White, bouncing in my brain "Word is bond," as I drive to work a double shift, and think of Frank White when he walks with his crew right into the mafia card game and grins, "Any nickle bag sold in the park I want in. You guys got fat while everyone starved on the street."

My wife is sleeping now, snoring a sober snore. She is a dark music I wear throughout the day. She is a 9 MM I carry in the holster of my chest. I touch her face lightly as she murmurs. When she was young, she used to run dope up from Ohio. Black tar they bought off the Mexican crews. She used to be state karate champion. She could drop you with an open palm. Now near forty, after ravaged years from alcoholism and disease, she gets up each day and drinks and makes our daughter's breakfast of fry bread and powdered sugar. She goes to her appointments. She buys potatoes. She writes some lines when she can. She braids our daughter's hair. She is a space between us that has grown. But tonight, she is a sober dreamer for the first time in longer than I can remember. The doctors tell her time is passing. She is trying, despite the wreckage. Isn't that all we can ask of the damned? The days that remain dwindle. I inhale the warm wind through the open window this summer as if it could be our last before the long procession into that other country. I keep the bagpipes at bay. I memorize our shadows in the long light of every evening. The ceiling fan turns its spiral in the blue light of the room. Across the city of AM, the last Ubers roll toward the doorways of dealers. The poppies lay down their sleepy heads.

I do not know what more to tell except with all our flaws and fractures we are the living.

David Caruso gave up acting to become an art dealer. I can't tell from Google if he actually paints. I don't care enough to look more. Horatio is about to solve the case. Did you know David Caruso's first "acting job" was posing as the "other guy" in police lineups? Perhaps that is the metaphor for my entire life: I have been the guy they hire to pretend they are the mugger, the forger, the rapist, the serial killer, the one who looks like the guy who did it for the witness to not finger. Because if they do, we know the suspect may be innocent. And when do the detectives ever want the suspect to be innocent?

What more can the poem do? O Love, did you know that Czeslaw Milosz was right when he argued, "What is poetry that does not save nations or people?"

You are my nation. I only wanted to write poems to save you.

Notes

"For I was hungry, and you gave me something to eat" is from the New Testament, Matthew 25:35.

Apoteka is a pharmacy chain in the Balkans.

The photos of Eastern European Jews from across Eastern Europe and particularly in the Carpathian region that this work engages were taken by Roman Vishniac in the late 1930s. The region is where my maternal great-grandparents, Hungarian speaking Jews, emigrated from in 1912. My grandfather visited our remaining European relatives when he was a boy in the 1930s. He would tell me, "They were all peasants. One was a violin maker." The entire extended family was executed during the Shoah.

Mark Rothko was an American painter known for his intensely spiritual exploration of color.

Azrael is the Hebrew angel who retrieves and guides the dead.

Sisyphus is a Greek myth. Sisyphus is condemned by the gods to push a stone forever up a hill, then watch it fall, only to have to push it up the next hill, and on and on for eternity, but what I often return to is the reconception of this myth by Albert Camus who posits that when the stone is released, there is a moment of freedom.

The veil is a reference to the thin places spoken of in ancient Irish Christianity and Celtic texts. It also plays off the Sufi idea of an endless third world which exists right beside our own, made of a leftover piece of clay from Creation the size of a sesame seed, between heaven and earth. More simply the veil is a notion of a place between light and shadow, part of the landscape of third-shift work, of the space between the living and the dead.

A Golem is a mythical creature made of clay that, it is written, could be invoked by a Rabbi during times of persecution.

Ginsberg is the poet Allen Ginsberg. Johnny Cash was an American Country singer.

Keith Jarret is an American Jazz Musician. The Jacksons were an American R&B group.

Elvis Costello is a British singer-songwriter. The Parliaments were a legendary American funk group. Gabarek is Jan Gabarek, a Swedish Jazz musician.

Adagio in G Minor is a classical composition by Tomaso Giovanni Albinoni.

Donkey Kong is a video game. Wile E. Coyote is a Looney Toons cartoon character.

Karen Fiser was a disabled poet from Boston. Her poem mentioned is titled "Wheelchairs that Kneel Down Like Elephants."

Some of the languages in these poems are my ancestral Yiddish, Hungarian, and Hebrew.

Van Morrison is a legendary Irish singer.

Jeff Buckley was an American rock singer known for his ethereal voice.

Alejandra Pizarnik was a 20th century Argentine poet of Polish Jewish heritage. She died by suicide in 1972.

All the etymologies in *My eleven-year-old daughter asks me for a pill* were simply gathered from the OED online and other common sources. They are in no way meant to be original research.

Milosz is the Polish poet Czelow Milosz.

The many therapies referenced in this book are imagined.

Acknowledgments

Gratitude to the editors of the following journals who first published some of these pieces. sometimes under different titles:

9 Mile Literary Review: "Whatever Happened to David Caruso," "The Hardest Part," "The Familiar Things of this World";
Barnstorm: "I'd Love to Have Been a Farmer";
Bennington Review: "Fugue of Four Suicides";
Bitter Oleander: "Hasidim Brooklyn Light";
Brevity: "Poem Woven with Birds and Grass After Long Hospital Stay";
Descant: "Eleven";
Diode: "After Tolstoy";
Heavy Feather Review: "Biscuits";
Hobart: "When Things Repeat";
Identity Theory: "Eulogy at my Own Wake After the Golden Girls";
The Laurel Review: "The Shape of a Pill";
San Pedro River Review: "Poem that Starts with a Photo of a Woman Faraway Walking through the Carpathian Hills";
Solstice Literary Review: "Frida Kahlo";
Southern Indiana Review: "I Have so Little to Offer this World";
Spoonie: "One Sentence on Pain";
Trasna (Ireland): "Braille";
Zin Dailey (Croatia): "A Window."

Thank you especially to the many folks who gave me encouragement, to Jeffrey McDaniel, Alicia Stallings, Martin Espada, Terrance Hayes, Julie Babcock, Dwayne Betts, Joe Weil and Emily Vogel, Peter Conners, Al Abonado,

Grace Bauer, Terry Blawkhawk, Laure-Anne Bosselaar, Kenny Carroll, Kevin Casey, Charles Cote, Daniel Donaghy, Michael Dumanis, Cheryl Dumesnil, Robert Fanning, Sarah Freligh, Carolyn Forché, George Franklin, Jennifer Franklin, John Gallaher, Brian Gilmore, Maria Mazziotti Gillan, Ani Gjika, Sherine Gilmour, Tony Gloeggler, Ximena Gomez, Peter Grandbois, George Guida, Justin Hamm, Bob Hass, Bob Herz, Le Hinton, Luisa A. Igloria, Richard Krawiec, Stephen Kuusisto, Michael Lally, Dorianne Laux, Adrian Matejka, Dinty Moore, Rachel Morgan, January Gil O'Neil, Phil Memmer, Phil Metres, Marjorie Maddox, Steve Myers, Jose Padua, Oliver de la Paz, Connie Post, Paul Roth, Luke Rolfes, Matthew Carey Salyer, Jeremy Shraffenberger, Natalie Solmer, John Richard Smith, William Stobb, Tim Suermondt, Jennifer K. Sweeney, Barbara Ungar, Jessica Walsh, Marcus Wicker, and the one and only Silvana Straw. And a whole lot more folks whose kindnesses small and large kept me going.

About the Author

Sean Thomas Dougherty is the author or editor of twenty books. His book *The Dead are Everywhere Telling Us Things* received the 2021 Jacar Press Poetry prize selected by Nickole Brown and Jessica Jacobs. His book *Not All Saints* won the 2020 Bitter Oleander Library of Poetry Prize. His book *The Second O of Sorrow* (BOA Editions, 2018) received both the Paterson Poetry Prize, and the Housatonic Book Award from Western Connecticut State University. Other awards include an Established Artist Fellowship for North-west Pennsylvania, the James Hearst Poetry Prize from North American Review, two Pennsylvania Council for the Arts Fellowships in Poetry, and a United States Fulbright Lectureship to the Balkans.

Sean's work as an editor includes the anthology *Alongside We Travel: Contemporary Poems on Autism* published by NYQ Books. This anthology was the first literary anthology to engage the complicated disability of Autism.

Sean currently works as a writing mentor with the MFA program in creative writing at Western Connecticut State University, and as a Medical Technician and long-term caregiver for folks with traumatic brain injuries. He was the seventh official poet laureate of Erie County, Pennsylvania.

BOA Editions, Ltd. American Poets Continuum Series

141

Colophon

BOA Editions, Ltd., a not-for-profit publisher of poetry and other literary works, fosters readership and appreciation of contemporary literature. By identifying, cultivating, and publishing both new and established poets and selecting authors of unique literary talent, BOA brings high-quality literature to the public.

Support for this effort comes from the sale of its publications, grant funding, and private donations.

~

The publication of this book is made possible, in part, by the special support of the following individuals:

Anonymous
Nelson Adrian Blish
Angela Bonazinga & Catherine Lewis
Susan Burke, *in honor of Boo Poulin*
Christopher C. Dahl
James Long Hale
Margaret B. Heminway
Charles Hertrick & Joan Gerrity
Grant Holcomb
Nora A. Jones
Paul LaFerriere & Dorrie Parini, *in honor of Bill Waddell*
Jack & Gail Langerak
Barbara Lovenheim
Joe McElveney
Daniel M. Meyers, *in honor of J. Shepard Skiff*
The Mountain Family, *in support of poets & poetry*
Nocon & Associates
Boo Poulin
John H. Schultz
Sue Stewart, *in memory of Stephen L. Raymond*
Robert Tortorella
Lee Upton, *in memory of Brittany Upton Cantrell*
William Waddell & Linda Rubel
Bruce & Jean Weigl